CHICAGO'S
BEST DIVE BARS
DRINKING AND DIVING IN THE WINDY CITY

Jonathan Stockton

Photography by Will Okun

Ig Publishing

Published by Gamble Guides
Gamble Guides is an imprint of Ig Publishing
178 Clinton Avenue
Brooklyn, NY 11205
www.igpub.com
igpublishing@earthlink.net

10 9 8 7 6 5 4 3 2 1

Book Interior design by Dayna Navaro

Dedicated to Adam Carr, for his steadfast support.

Old Town Ale House

CHICAGO'S BEST DIVE BARS
(arranged by neighborhood)

Club Foot

Introduction

I first knew Chicago as a city of skyscrapers. Riding in from Milwaukee with my mother, I would search for the Sears Tower, a steel mountain in the prairie, and as it grew on the horizon, I fixed my eyes upon it, oblivious to the neighborhoods that spread north, west and south. Chicago was downtown, where people lived and worked in the sky.

Those curtains of glass, concrete and steel still inspire awe. But that's postcard Chicago—tour buses and department stores. To uncover this city, I had to leave the Loop—and not just for "safe" neighborhoods like Lincoln Park, Wicker Park or Lake View. I had to follow the streets to where the lights on the great masts atop the Sears Tower look like low, blinking stars. I wanted to meet real Chicagoans, with all their accents and colors, on their terms, on their turf. And I found them in the city's dive bars.

In the year spent compiling this guide, I drank at more than 180 bars, and from those I picked 93 dives in 45 neighborhoods as the "best." I went diving on weeknights—after my nine-to-five—on weekends and on holidays. On bad nights, when I was cranky and worn out, I dragged myself to bars. On good nights I skipped down the street. I once sat in the driver's seat, my hands shaking with fear, trying to muster the courage to leave the car. I heard stories that made me laugh till it hurt. I saw a man get a blow job. I toured the West Side with an ex-con who did time for manslaughter and saw women prostitute themselves to buy crack. I received advice. A stranger prayed for me. I met a saint. I got very, very drunk.

Chicago's Best Dive Bars is surely flawed. Some of the bars described here are too froufrou to be dives, others are out-and-out dangerous. I ignored some neighborhoods and gave others far too much attention. But if this book doesn't include every dive, it contains most, from classics like the Old Town Ale House and Velvet Lounge to obscure shacks such as Domino, or the slew of South Side Naugahyde lounges.

Dive bars are disappearing. According to a June 13, 2004, article in the *Tribune,* Chicago once had 6,979 taverns. These days, you'll find about 1,300, down from 3,299 in 1990. Reasons for this decline vary—from political agendas to changing attitudes about drinking. Whatever the reasons, now is the time to dive.

What makes a bar a dive?

Dive bars are old and broken. The padding on the stools is ripped. Duct tape holds the cooler door to its hinges. Signs are burned out or faded, and the toilets smell of urine, the floors beneath them rotted from years of overflow. Mirrors are cracked, the paint a flaky mess. A can of roach killer is in open view.

Dive bars are named for their owners, living or dead (Norma's, Michelle's, Bernice & John's). Spelling and grammar suffers (Crabbby Kim's, Ed & Jeans). Puns are popular (Drop Inn Lounge, Sue's Wok On Inn Bar Kitchen). So is the theme of heavy drinking (Hangovers, Rich's First One Today). And if liquor is on the sign (Rothschild's Liquor Mart), you've likely found a dive.

At dives you see all sorts. At Billy Goat Tavern, reporters congregate at the end of the bar while tourists sit at tables with their shopping bags. Iron workers joke inside the Sea of Happiness, and at Loop Tavern, a man sells socks out of a garbage bag. At Cal's, a trader rolls up his sleeves and stares into his beer. Couples step dance at Bob's Place Lounge. A drunk falls. A jazz legend nods off. A son announces his mom's birthday.

There's something intangible about a good dive—more than cheap booze and coarseness, stale pretzels and shouting matches. It's a pat on the back from someone you've never met, a bartender who buys the round, an invitation to dance from a woman twice your age. Something tips the balance to make a bar not just a bar, but a dive bar. When you've plunged into a dive, you just know it.

Dive ratings

The bars in this book are rated from 1 to 10:

1 ●
Suitable for small children.

5 ●●●●●
Take note of the quickest escape routes.

10 ●●●●●●●●●●
You haven't lived if you haven't faced death.

Pinball Dives
The Cove
Club Foot
Hungry Brain
Lakeview Lounge
Lincoln Square Lanes
Old Town Ale House
Phyllis's Musical Inn

Chicago's ten best dives
(in alphabetical order)

1. **New Apartment Lounge**—*three bars in one, must-see Tuesday jazz*

2. **The V.I.P.**—*amateur, take your bitch ass back to Riptide*

3. **Rossi's**—*drink your breakfast*

4. **Rothschild's Liquor Mart**—*buzzer bathrooms*

5. **Ed and Jeans**—*dive bar diorama, no ice*

6. **Cunneen's Tavern**—*great music, great everything*

7. **Michelle's**—*beautiful people*

8. **The Sea of Happiness**—*downtown savior*

9. **Old Town Ale House**—*legendary*

10. **Bernice & John's**—*my Bridgeport hideaway*

Lakeview Lounge

WEST

AUSTIN
LAWNDALE
GARFIELD PARK

American Legion Hall #1268

3918 W. Roosevelt Road (Lawndale)
773-722-4097

Hours: 3 p.m.–11 p.m., Sunday-Thursday; 3 p.m.–2 a.m.,
Friday and Saturday
Forest Park Blue Line to Pulaski then transfer to
the southbound #53 Pulaski bus

Police tape flapped in the biting February wind, and the only illumination came through the front windows of a corner liquor store. I hurried down an unshoveled icy sidewalk to the door of American Legion Hall #1268. It was locked. I buzzed and waited nervously—Lawndale can be scary at night—but when the door opened, I was drenched with music, warmth and light. I had stumbled upon a party: bluesman Little Arthur Duncan had turned seventy.

Despite his potbelly and advanced age, Duncan still had moves. Wild wavy hair shot out from under his hat, and he stalked the crowd like a cat in heat, growling right into our faces. Other singers followed, including a black woman who bellowed about sleeping with her white husband, a "cracker," and a man whose maroon leather suit smelled like a new car.

The hall's full name is Crispus Attucks American Legion Hall #1268, after the black sailor and rope maker shot at the Boston Massacre, the first man killed in the American Revolution. A picture of him above the bar is flanked by photographs of the Legion's founders. The hall serves as a club for local black war veterans. Most nights expect a largely African American crowd. A flyer advertised dancing at 5 p.m. on every third Tuesday of the month with music by Smooth D.

I took in the whole scene from my seat at the bar, drinking my $2 High Life while devouring generous portions of corn bread, greens, rib tips and deviled eggs. (Don't expect food on most nights, though.) As I stabbed at my meal with a plastic fork, next to me sat Reverend Willie Guest, sleeves pulled up, attacking dinner with his hands. He plays piano, he says, and in the '60s his band wrote "Shake Your Tail Feather." He complained he had never earned a cent in royalties. The Reverend may have had some gripes, but sitting at the Legion, my lips sticky from the soul food, my head filled with beer and the blues, I had none.

Dive Rating: 8 ● ● ● ● ● ● ● ●

Lady Di's Pad

The Green Line's Laramie stop is to the south, but driving is highly recommended.

I arrived at Lady Di's Pad in style, tucked away in Big Ol Pimp's extra-large SUV, unsettled only by the fact that the back doors could only be opened from the outside. After being let out, I followed B.O.P. to the club's side entrance, an anonymous door in a windowless brick wall. (The proprietor, Diane, keeps the front door locked because of frequent armed stick-ups). Behind me followed Tony, B.O.P.'s quiet older brother. "Don't worry," Tony said. "He got your front. I got your back."

Inside the bartender, a lady in a smart suit coat, greeted B.O.P. from behind the kidney-shaped bar. I ordered a gin and tonic, but B.O.P., who paid all night, would not allow it. "You're a brown liquor man," he said. "You got to have something brown." The bartender pulled out a bottle of Old Grand-Dad, and after B.O.P. checked to make sure the bourbon was genuine 100 proof, he ordered her to pour me a glass. While brownbibing, I noticed that Lady Di's Pad has some of the coolest bar-chitecture around, ideal for a Snoop Dogg video. The cocktail tables, cut from marbled Formica and stratified in oddly shaped layers, look like canyon walls worn down by centuries of bar rags and spilled drinks. In the back, fabulous curved walls of white stone swallow up a dance floor that is lit from beneath. An adjacent room has a full bar and islands surrounded by stools and is used to host DJ battles and R&B acts. For now, live music has been stopped.

Lady Di's Pad also has a video slot machine. I asked B.O.P, whose colorful history includes drug dealing, strip show promotions and a few years in Joliet for attempted murder, if he knew anything about the video slot machine racket. (Lots of bars have them, but I had never understood their appeal.) B.O.P. said that some bars illegally pay out the customer winnings. Apparently the slots are mob owned, and when the toughs come round to collect their quarters, they reimburse the bar for whatever it has paid out to the winners that week.

According to Big Ol' Pimp, Lady Di's Pad used to be the spot, until frequent fighting scared customers away. Now, as at many other black clubs, customers younger than thirty are not particularly welcome. As B.O.P. says, "Young people start trouble and don't buy nothing."

Dive Rating: 10 ●●●●●●●●●●

Bossman Blues Center   3500 W. Lake Street (Garfield Park)
773-722-8744

Hours: noon–2 a.m., Sunday-Friday; noon–3 a.m., Saturday
Green Line to Conservatory–Central Park Drive

Bossman Blues Center is clean and bright these days, as a major face-lift has replaced the old, caged windows with the tinted, floor-to-ceiling storefront sort. The bar is painted bright blue, and adorned with a bronze bust of Mozart (?). Though not thoroughly modern, this uncluttered space could easily pass for a new coffeehouse. As a matter of fact, I didn't think BBC was a dive until an old man wearing a snowsuit, cowboy boots and a tie took the microphone and started wailing.

BBC is across the street from picturesque Garfield Park, with its lagoons, gold dome and botanical gardens. But don't let the greenery fool you: this neighborhood is rugged and rough. Garfield Park (Police District 11) frequently tops monthly police reports for most homicides, this in a city that last year lead the country in murders.

In this case a little thing like death shouldn't scare you away. While the world outside BBC may tip a bit toward urban nightmare, the world inside is safe and full of charismatic characters eager to meet you, even if you may not be as eager to meet them. One man counted off all the women he'd slept with who weighed more than he did. (And he didn't have the body of an athlete.) Another tried to sell me kitchen appliances. And I (and everyone else) was repeatedly asked by the band to come up and play. I declined, but others took the open invitation, and man those cats could wail. Meanwhile I talked to Bossman, who wore a florescent orange crossing guard vest as he told tales of the blues' past. Among the best of his nuggets was one about how he witnessed—as a kid looking through a club window—the night B. B. King was given his nickname. He also gave me a piece of advice: "You don't go to a Japanese restaurant for Italian food, so don't go to the Northside for blues. Go to Bossman Blues Center."

Dive Rating: 7 ●●●●●●●

Bossman Blues Center

Charlie's Bar

5471 W. Division Street (Austin)
773-261-9889

Hours: 2 p.m.–2 a.m., Sunday-Friday; 2 p.m.–3 a.m., Saturday
#70 Division or the #85 Central bus

Charlie's Bar has an ingenious method for keeping customers at the bar—the promise of free food. After spotting Charlie's twinkling lights, I pulled off Division Street and parked my car. Out back three men stood over a smoking grill. Meats hissed, and I asked what was cooking. They said chicken and ribs for Charlie's Bar. I was hungry and, with the promise of free grub, I went in. It was 8 p.m. I sat at the J-shaped bar across from a man who ate pork rinds with hot sauce. Tables by the dance floor displayed ketchup, pickle spears and pre-sliced white bread, all signs of what I was certain was an upcoming BBQ feast.

As Charlie's filled, people started dancing, while the DJ, perched in his booth, looked through large binoculars, checking the score of the Bulls game. A woman hung a plastic ring with pinchers above her group's table. A few dollars were added to it; someone tacked on a ten. I asked the woman what was going on. "It's a money tree," she said. "It's my auntie's birthday. Are you going to put some money up?" I chipped in a buck. She demanded I buy her a beer. (Sorry, lady . . . you can ask, but don't demand.) I waited. I sucked down several $2 Millers. I waited some more. I pondered the worn party decorations (shriveled balloons) and ragged Happy Birthday sign (for auntie?). And I waited.

I starved. At midnight I gave up my wait, tipped my bartender and rushed out, flooring my seventy-one horses to the nearest taco stand. Charlie, the owner, still claims his bar serves BBQ. I don't believe him.

Dive Rating: 7 ●●●●●●●

Charlie's Bar

Esquire Lounge

Esquire Lounge

4905 W. Madison Street (Austin)
773-921-8160
Hours: noon–2 a.m., Sunday-Friday; noon–3 a.m., Saturday
#20 Madison Street bus or ride the Green Line to Cicero and walk south
toward Madison Street (And be careful out there.)

On the wild West Side of Chicago, whole blocks of streetlights go dark. Groups of kids play fight on corners well past midnight. Motorists stop where they like—middle of the road, middle of the intersection—and breeze through red lights. Cops speed by, engines roaring. A friend who grew up in the West Side projects says his buddies carried baseball bats in their cars. When a man strayed off the sidewalk and walked in the street—even if he was right by the curb—they'd drive up real close and, as they passed, someone would lean out the window with the bat and swing.

Picture all of this when you roll up to the Esquire Lounge on W. Madison Street. If driving, park in the car park adjacent to the lounge—that area fenced in by razor wire and corrugated steel. Before you get out of your car, think to yourself: everybody in this bar will know I'm alone, I am not from around here, and no one's got my back. Then leave those thoughts in the car, because everything is going to be cool.

The first time I stopped at Esquire was with B.O.P.—Big Ol' Pimp—a former gangbanger gone straight. I arrived drunk and remember little, only that B.O.P. dubbed the Esquire crowd "good people"—business owners, city employees and professionals. And maybe the occasional thug. On my second and more sober stop, I sat next to two men playing dominoes as a woman with Pam Grier caliber charisma tended bar. Occasionally a regular would join her, fetching his own beer and a couple more for his friends. Some ladies had rolled down from Milwaukee and let the bar know it, shaking ass and commanding men to buy them drinks. Along a wall of mirrors, a woman celebrated her birthday as people stuffed congratulatory greenbacks into her miniature lottery basket. A group played cards in the corner. A DJ spun R&B.

Between the smiles, jokes and general laughter, someone pulled a gun on me—a snub-nosed plastic squirt gun. The woman who pulled it saluted me, saying I needed a partner (an insinuation that I must be a cop.) We danced a few steps as the night edged toward its end.

Dive Rating: 8

The Marquis Room

5065 W. Madison Street (Austin)

*Hours: 11 a.m.–2 a.m., Monday-Friday; 11 a.m.–3 a.m.,
Saturday; noon-midnight, Sunday
#20 Madison bus (Packing a weapon suggested)*

A bit scary to (white) strangers, the Marquis certainly has the classic dive bar look down cold. Vinyl covers everything, and mock roofs form darling little overhangs on the walls. The carpet is a dark, ragged mess. The dance floor in back has a shadowy grid, and a geometric stain from when it used to light up from beneath. Crossing the ceiling are what look like two giant air ducts. They are covered in red plastic and, in a West Side kind of way, suggest the famous angled I-beams that clamber up the John Hancock Center.

White people rarely walk into this bar, and if they do, they are either escorted by black friends or carry a badge. I came alone, and when I sat down, the man nearest to me—a good four feet away—slid his chair further away to show I was not wanted. Four young women sat to my left. I smiled at them. They went quiet. I ordered an Old Style ($1) and a shot of Jim Beam. I got a can and three fingers of bourbon in a cocktail glass.

After a while nature called, and I asked the man who had scooted away—in my whitest voice—"Excuse me, could you direct me to the toilet?" The man said nothing, but his arm rose slowly from his side with the index finger extended. I followed its aim to the rear of the tavern. Two doors blended into the wall. On one of the doors was painted, in a worn golden script, "Powder Room." On the other, "Alley Cats."

In Alley Cats I fumbled for a lock (there was none), then turned to the urinal to find a flushing handle but no basin. Next to it was a toilet that had been attacked by a shark. Half the seat had survived. As I attended to business and looked over the gang symbols carved into the wall, fresh air seeped in through the cracks of the boarded up window, reviving my senses. I finished and pulled the handle. No flush. After some twisting, I convinced the moaning tap to spit out some water.

Back in the bar, I tried my best to blend in. When that failed, I strolled to the end of the bar, faking interest in the ballgame on television. Seeing this, the bartender also strolled across the length of the bar . . . and extinguished the TV set. I was left to chat with a patron who, luckily for me, had stored up a week's worth of conversation. After introductions, she released a torrent of words that drowned whatever sense the breeze in the bathroom had just revived. Against the deafening flow, I tried to get in a few "excuse me's" and "could you repeat that's?" but it was no use. I left her in mid-sentence and went back to my barstool. There awaited my beer and my bourbon. And Cocoa.

Cocoa and I got to talking. I told her about the bar book I was writing, and she detailed her college plans. She would pursue two degrees: one in the culinary arts, the other in graphic design. I asked her if the two degrees seemed a little unrelated. She said: "I love to cook. Cooking is what I am. But I've always wanted to be a graphic designer. That's what I want. If one doesn't work out, I can always fall back on the other." The ambitious Cocoa soon demanded my telephone number in case neither degree worked out. One of them must have. She still hasn't called.

Dive Rating: 10 ⬤⬤⬤⬤⬤⬤⬤⬤⬤⬤

Liquor Stores
Cal's
Hangovers
Kaplan's Liquors
Loop Tavern
Moon's Bar & Liquor
Ola's Liquors
Rothschild's Liquor Mart
Tap Room

The V.I.P.

5065 W. Madison Street (Austin)
773-626-8602
Hours: 11 a.m.–2 a.m., Monday-Friday; 11 a.m.–3 a.m.,
Saturday; noon-midnight, Sunday
#20 Madison bus

A lady who calls the V.I.P. her second home told me she rarely sees white people here, especially without the "proper escort." A fat man put it more bluntly: "You couldn't have come here fifteen years ago. You'd been robbed. Or maybe shot." Despite these warnings, the V.I.P. is not an unfriendly place, certainly more welcoming than its neighbor, the Marquis Room, with which it shares a wall, side door and liquor license.

My one and only evening here was quite a blast. A man sang along with Marvin Gaye on the microphone as a gritty woman named Monique dropped pearls of knowledge to me and anyone else who would listen. "Using people's one thing," she mused. "Misusing people's another thing. A lot of people don't know the difference." The curvy bartender was dressed in tight black leather, a studded black motorcycle cap tilted atop her head.

The V.I.P. comes adorned with some of the most essential fixtures of any self-loathing dive bar—cheap wood paneling, dim (burnt-out) lighting, and after-three-drinks-on-the-rocks-who-gives-a-fuck-colored ceilings, as one regular noted. Behind the bar are makeshift shelves, liquor bottles, knickknacks and cans of roach and ant killer. Taped to the cash register, a sign read: "If you need credit, you don't need a drink. You need a job."

After a few hours and more than a few well-mixed drinks, my night came to an end. As I got up to leave, I thought that even though I didn't feel completely accepted by the crowd, at least I hadn't been robbed or shot. I could see the bar manager in back, fast asleep in a comfy leather chair, undisturbed by the clamor around him. It was a sweet sight, but inconsistent with my first image of him, when, a few hours earlier, he had barked at me to come speak with him, then barked permission for me to speak with his customers. Watching him rest under his baseball cap, I resisted the temptation to kiss his forehead, and extinguish all the lights.

Dive Rating: 10 ●●●●●●●●●●

FAR NORTH

ANDERSONVILLE

EDGEWATER

ROGERS PARK

Cunneen's Tavern

1424 W. Devon Avenue (Rogers Park)
773-274-9317

Hours: noon–2 a.m., Sunday-Friday; noon–3 a.m., Saturday
The Red Line to Loyola, then either walk or take the westbound #155
Devon Ave. bus

At Cunneen's Tavern one night, I encountered a Buffalo native who marked as the highlight of his life the night he smoked PCP at a Roger Waters show and woke up the next morning on a highway median. Since then, his dream was to start a lounge act that covered heavy metal songs and toured airports, and he firmly believed that Ween's "Polka Dot Tail" was written about his life. In a nutshell, that is Cunneen's, a place where the music comes first and life's realities a distant second. And, fortunately for the former, you'll never hear better music at a bar, as the bartenders pick from the owner's substantial record collection ("There's even more in back," one told me). You won't hear the latest hits, but they'll play old dusties that will blow your mind even more than the PCP did Mr. Polka Dot Tail's.

Most nights you can find a seat at Cunneen's, though on Thursdays during the school year the place is overrun with Loyola University students. Prices are modest: a pint of Berghoff lager costs $2.50, a pitcher $8. This is also a purebred Chicago bar, proud bearer of our four-star flag. Memorabilia includes photographs of the city after the Great Fire, a replica of an old saloon license and the framed front page showing Chicagoans celebrating the end of Prohibition. (We celebrate still.) From an old clock above the bar, Boss Daley glares down Pharaoh-like over the crowd, forever assured he'll get the votes. Take your time in the toilets, as the cartoon display cases are great, and the funnies are refreshed each week.

On a recent stop, a Miller commercial came on the television, one in which a High Life man builds a hot dog. For some reason, this innocuous ad really pissed off the bartender. "I'm suing Miller Brewing Company," she quipped. "Not only for taking over Old Style beer but for putting fucking ketchup on a hotdog. In Chicago, we do it with mustard." And in Cunneen's, they do it with music.

Dive Rating: 4 ●●●●

Granville Anvil

1137 W. Granville Avenue (Edgewater)
773-973-0006

Hours: 7 a.m.–2 a.m., Monday-Friday; 7 a.m.–3 a.m., Saturday;
noon–2 a.m., Sunday
Red Line to Granville

You may already know this, but being gay doesn't necessarily mean you have taste. The Anvil seems especially determined to crush this high-style stereotype. Its arsenal includes laughable charcoal drawings of men in leather (biker caps, hairy abs) and videos of orgies in the woods. Two plaster penises of intimidating dimensions, one drooping sadly, the other suitable for hanging a cocktail party's worth of coats on, loom over the men's room door. And, a 100-plus-pound iron anvil used to sit on a pedestal just inside the bar's door. Until someone stole it.

Despite the lapses in interior décor, the Anvil can be a hell of a lot of fun. The $3.75 dirty gin martinis are a potent steal, and the furry sweetheart (flannel shirt with no sleeves and a tangle of chest hair) who served it made me smile each time he called me darling. In summer the deck is open, and, FYI, the 7 a.m. bartender goes by the name of Feathers. The Anvil is also ethnically diverse and an easy place to strike up a conversation. And get hit on. Several thousand times, I had to ask the banker who sat next to me to remove his hands from my shoulders and knee. Between sips of martini, he invented elaborate schemes to get me to exit my closet and enter his nearby apartment.

If you like horror, talk to Al the bartender. He worked here when the bar was called Irish Mike's Terrace. One morning in 1974, he arrived at work to find the previous night's bartender murdered. The victim's hands had been tied behind his back, he had been stabbed multiple times in the chest, and his throat had been slit.

Dive Rating: 8

DJs Ranch

6962 N. Glenwood Avenue (Rogers Park)
773-764-6088

Hours: 4:30 p.m.–2 a.m., Monday-Saturday; 4:30 p.m.–1 a.m., Sunday
Red Line north to Morse, then walk a couple of blocks north on
Glenwood Ave. Glenwood runs on both sides of the El tracks.
Take the street west of the tracks.

Mike, owner/bartender at DJs Ranch, summarizes the history of his place as follows: "This was once a piano bar, once an Irish bar, once a biker bar, and once hell on a stick, with every drugged-up person you could think of." Then Mike came in, started turning away the Rogers Park roughnecks and hood rats, and raised the bar's drinking age to twenty-five. "For every person that comes here, there's two people barred," he says with obvious pride.

Despite Mike's efforts, DJs Ranch still looks like hell on a stick. The paint on the walls is long past disintegration, and the main clientele seem to be video slot addicts. An abused dartboard hangs on to a ratty piece of carpet, and the bathrooms are crooked shacks. The last time I was there, I sat down next to a drunken security guard who promptly began yelling about his job, ticket prices at Cubs games and what I'd better do with my life.

And yet I can recommend DJs Ranch because of one thing, one man— Mike. He is a great guy who makes a mean dirty martini and drinks from a jewel-encrusted goblet that reads, "TADOW." The goblet alone is worth a trip. The Ranch also hosts DJs most Fridays and some Saturdays (rap, R&B, soul), and the big game is always on the TV. Feel free to quiz Mike on sports. He knows them all.

Dive Rating: 7 ⚫⚫⚫⚫⚫⚫

DJs Ranch

Jackhammer

Hours: 4 p.m.–4 a.m., Monday-Friday; 2 p.m.–5 a.m., Saturday;
2 p.m.–4 a.m., Sunday
#22 Clark Street bus

FAR NORTH

I stormed into Jackhammer expecting filth and depravity. Instead I found cowboys in ironed blue jeans and drag queens in sashes, dancing to Top 20 country music. What the hell was going on? Then I found out about the Windy City Rodeo, a gay rodeo held each year some 50 miles south of the city. The cowboys and beauty queens had come up from the rodeo and were hopping along from gay bar to gay bar, having some good old prairie fun and encouraging the locals to head south for some entertainment in the dust and sun. The troop was a hit for the brief time they were there, but sadly they had to mosey along, and when they left, the tumbleweeds started to blow through Jackhammer.

That, I gather, sums up Jackhammer—dead one moment, a raging party the next. If you're gay, know that the drinks are cheap ($1 beers on Thursday) and the action hot. If you're straight, you'll want to skip this one. Television monitors often broadcast gay porn, and a little stage with a pole welcomes visiting strippers. There is also a pool table and an entrance to what apparently is the basement, which was chained shut. When I asked Iron Man—my pool partner, whose short shorts showed off his shaved legs—why the door was chained, he told me that the police had closed it, temporarily, as some men were doing "bad, dirty things down there."

Dive Rating: 6 ●●●●●●

CHICAGO'S BEST DIVE BARS

Jarheads

6973 N. Clark Street (Rogers Park)
773-973-1907
Hours: 4 p.m.–midnight, Daily
#22 Clark bus or take the Red Line to Morse and walk west

Few seem to have heard of Jarheads. Perhaps it's the camouflage. From the outside, this teensy tavern of white clapboard and green trim looks like someone's well-kept home. Inside you'll find General Patton's military wet dream. Real camouflage netting covers the ceiling, models of military airplanes and helicopters patrol the skies and a collection worthy of Rambo—military vests, packs, patches and pictures—adorns the walls. The place even smells like an army surplus store.

Despite the combative atmosphere, Jarhead's owner, John, a solid man with snow-white hair, is exceedingly cheerful. He laughs and jokes and shakes one hell of a hand. Still, if I were a stick-up man, I would pick another bar to rob. Of several signs warning of possible weapons, the most chilling cautions, "If you can read this you're in range." And a real, honest-to-god bazooka dangles above the bar, within easy reach.

Even the most picky drill sergeant would have difficulty finding fault with Jarheads. The old battle helmets, figurines and trinkets are kept dust free, and the hundred odd mounted photographs, plaques and pictures are hung as level as a good crew cut. Beer costs $2.50, and there are also darts and a well-oiled pinball machine.

Civilians are tolerated, though most visitors have served in the military, as one can tell from their mesh hats touting a certain ship or battalion, or their faded tattoos of eagles, flags and other patriotic symbols. You will also notice a collection for POW/MIAs behind the bar. And when old vets call it a night, they rarely leave without a hug. However, if you are Jane Fonda, or as one bumper sticker puts it, "American Traitor Bitch," you are advised to stay away.

Dive Rating: 3

Lakeview Lounge

5110 N. Broadway (Edgewater)
773-769-0994
Hours: 11 a.m.–4 a.m., Monday-Friday; 11 a.m.–5 a.m.,
Saturday; 5 p.m.–4 a.m., Sunday
Red Line to Argyle

There are two things wrong with the Lakeview Lounge. Drinks are too expensive. And it's not close to my apartment.

To be fair, the prices at this Edgewater (not Lake View) hole-in-the-wall aren't ridiculous, but a bottle of Old Style for $3.50? That's just not right. And rail cocktails for $4 isn't much better. Luckily, Nighthawk, the famed house band that plays Thursday through Sunday, 10 p.m. to 4 a.m., does so for free. Perched on the small stage decorated with tinsel and Christmas lights that sits behind the M-shaped bar, Nighthawk is a live jukebox, churning out pre-'80s hits from Roy Orbison to Creedence Clearwater Revival to The Eagles. I've heard them bang out a Johnny Cash medley (two, three times in the same evening), and the bassist/vocalist is not above futzing with the classics. Covering "Purple Haze," he belts out: "Excuse me while I kiss my ass." A machine that trickles out bubbles from the ceiling seems wildly modern, and when the guitarist turns it on the audience lights up.

The walls are paneled wood. Above the tables hang backlit landscapes of the North Woods, the photographs singed and cracked from the heat of the bulbs. The bathrooms are small but clean, and the men's stall is hilariously tiny. Its door is chest height and without a lock. When a man sits on the pot, his feet stick out and his hand grabs the bottom of the door to keep it from bursting open. I've seen that stall humble the toughest of customers.

The Lakeview Lounge is for drunks, and thankfully they're well taken care of by the staff. On Easter, Joe, described to me as a "silent partner," handed out pink and purple hard-boiled eggs. And when the man standing next to me passed out, the bartender kindly cleared out a spot for me and another guy to drag him to. She even made a pillow of his jacket.

The place frequently pops up in the Missed Connections section of the *Chicago Reader,* a place where Chicagoans too shy to ask someone out the first time try for a remember-me long shot. However, ads from the

Lounge are always a little different. A recent one read, "We met at the Lakeview Lounge. I went home with you. I left my flask at your place. I'm not interested in seeing you. I just really want my flask back."

Dive Rating: 6 ⬤⬤⬤⬤⬤⬤

Lakeview Lounge

Ollie's

Ollie's

1064 W. Berwyn Avenue (Edgewater)
773-784-5712

*Hours: 10 a.m.–10 p.m., Monday-Thursday; 10 a.m.–1 a.m.,
Friday and Saturday; 11 a.m.–9 p.m., Sunday
The Red Line to Berwyn and look east for the mug of Schlitz
with plenty of head*

Walk into Ollie's on a Saturday night and the person at the door makes you buy a token for $4. That token buys your first drink. The second drink you have to pay for with cash, and my second gin and tonic cost $4.20. A regular told me that prices are raised on the weekends, but I wanted to know, why charge such an odd price at all? Wouldn't four and a quarter make more sense? I asked Ollie, the owner, but she didn't see it my way.

Many more things befuddled me at Ollie's. Like how to get in. I approached from the nearby El stop to the west and tried two doors, which were locked. I was ready to give up after door number two when two men approached. I hid round the corner and watched as they peeked through the dark windows to see who was DJing. They popped into a third door, and I made my move. Inside, after the token ordeal and a gin tonic, I went to play pool. Fifteen names were on the list, and the long wait gave me just enough time to read the house rules for the pool table, three full sheets of them, in a font size that made me squint. I had also had time to ask one man why he had a bandage wrapped around his head. He said, in garbled English, that he had recently tripped over his bed in the dark and put his head through a wall. He really shouldn't have been drinking.

Ollie's has three sections: a bar, a sitting area and a dance floor. Tinted windows and black interior paint keep the bar dark, and the decorations are sparse, little more than painted silver musical notes and strings of colored lights. The crowd is mostly African American with a smattering of everything else.

Dive Rating: 6 ●●●●●●

Simon's

5210 N. Clark Street (Andersonville)
773-878-0894

Hours: 11 a.m.–2 a.m., Sunday-Friday; 11 a.m.–3 a.m., Saturday
#22 Clark Street bus or take the Red Line to the Berwyn stop

Simon's wasn't Simon Lundberg's first bar. Just his first legal one. Before opening Simon's in 1934—the year after Prohibition was lifted—Lundberg ran a speakeasy in the building's basement, the N&N (No Norwegians), and a café up the street that illegally spiked its coffee with whiskey. Lundberg, a Swede, built a bank in his new bar. At the time, two-fifths of the nation's banks had closed, and Chicagoans were cashing paychecks at local grocers and butcher shops that skimmed a percentage off the top. But Simon's cashed without charge and threw in a free sandwich. On paydays, Lundberg's bank netted him a crowd of thirsty men with cash in hand.

The little bank beneath the stairs cashed as much as $14,000 in a month, about $200,000 in today's money. To keep the money secure, Lundberg fitted the teller's window with bulletproof glass, its walls with sheets of twelve-gauge steel. Security measures included a hole drilled into the floor to slip rolls of silver dollars through, a buzzer to the upstairs apartment and trapdoor in the wall to restock the cash drawer.

When immigrant Swedes new to Chicago needed work, they were often directed to Simon's, where Lundberg would test their mettle by making them a driver for the night. Lundberg owned six bars, and as he made his nightly rounds, he would feed his new driver a shot and a beer at every stop. If his man were still steady after twelve drinks, Lundberg would see what he could do.

These days Simon's isn't run down, just worn in. An engraved mirror is cracked, and the "new" ceiling, installed in the '50s, is soiled yellow with cigarette smoke. At the far end of the bar, two stained-glass fish enjoy a drink above a fake fireplace and threadbare chairs. In this little nook, photos from the old days show parades and politicians back when bartenders dressed in white shirts, black ties and aprons. The bar sports a nautical theme, with portholes framed in mahogany, a sixty-foot cherry wood bar and mirrors engraved with illustrations of the stately SS Normandie, then the world's largest and most luxurious cruise ship. The bar's opulence never rivaled that of the boat, but Simon's still serves, while the SS Normandie was long ago stripped for scrap metal.

CHICAGO'S BEST DIVE BARS

And there's the mural. Painted in 1956 by local artist Sig Olson, it depicts one of Lundberg's wild hunting parties in Michigan. A lodge is surrounded by shy deer, green pastures and tranquil woods, but inside the lodge Lundberg and friends are in a frenzy for some reason. Inserted into all of this is a portrait of a creepy old man, which you can tell was not part of the original painting. Find current owner Scottie, and he'll tell you an amazing story about who was removed from the hunting party and why the old man replaced him.

There's live music on Sundays, and the jukebox has no equal. It's chock-a-block with the best of British rock: Small Faces, Zombies, Kinks and more. This may be Heath's doing, whose British Invasion band the New Invaders play the last Sunday of the month. Pabst on tap costs $2.50.

Dive Rating: 3 ⬤ ⬤ ⬤

Simon's

Touché

6412 N. Clark Street (Rogers Park)
773-465-7400
Hours: 5 p.m.–4 a.m., Monday-Friday; 3 p.m.–5 a.m.,
Saturday; 3 p.m.–4 a.m. Sunday
#22 Clark Street bus, or take the Red Line to Loyola and transfer to the
#155 Devon bus

FAR NORTH

Established in 1977 and situated next door to Jackhammer, Touché is one of the older gay bars around, and a Saturday night here is a lesson in things I've always suspected but never wanted to know.

The front room is pleasant enough, with a coat check run by a flaming queen who speaks only in sexual innuendo. He introduced me to two guys before I could say hello, and offered me candy if I couldn't find something else to suck on. I escaped, but I must say, I felt the bar's eyes upon me, as if I were the new piece of candy. I spoke to a few men to try to get comfortable, then downed a drink for courage and walked to the back room, where the real action is.

The back bar is painted black, and just inside this cavern you'll find a small rectangular cage. Black screens and a ladder of old car tires hang from the ceiling. Gay porn plays on the big screen as dance music thumps from the speakers.

CHICAGO'S BEST DIVE BARS

I am no fan of being touched by strangers—call it a hang up—but I like it even less when an unknown man built like a fullback starts kneading my ass. Such a feel was copped as another man at the bar explained how I was "datable." I asked him if the fullback who grabbed my ass was as datable as me. "No, but I would suck his dick and lick his balls and have him cum in my face then rub it in my hair and be all dirty and not wash it out until I got home," he said, adding, "That would be hot." He talked to me like this for an hour, divulging information with a frankness that was difficult to believe. He matter-of-factly explained how he had recently been fucked in one of Touché's dark corners, and that he'd love to be fucked right out in the open, with the whole bar watching. Again, "That would be so hot." Occasionally he would pull condoms and packets of lubrication from his pockets and tell me he was drunk.

I returned to the front room, where there's a pool table, darts and brighter lights, to take a breather and drink a $1.50 draft beer. A conversation with the man next to me led to travel, and he told me about

Amsterdam. I asked what he liked better, the drugs or the prostitutes. He said, "I just like to walk through the red light district and see what straight people have to pay for."

Touché is also home to the Great Lakes Bears, a community of robust, hairy gays. Membership meetings start at 9 p.m. on the first Saturday of the month. And lastly, if using the men's room, know there's a mirror attached to the ceiling above the urinals so those waiting behind can inspect your equipment.

Dive Rating: 8 ●●●●●●●●

Gay Dives
Granville Anvil
Jackhammer
Lost & Found (lesbian)
Second Story Bar
Touché

Red Line Tap

7006 N. Glenwood Avenue (Rogers Park)
773-338-9862

*Hours: 4 p.m.–2 a.m., Monday-Friday; 11 a.m.–3 a.m.,
Saturday; 11 a.m.–2 p.m., Sunday
Red Line to Morse and walk north. Glenwood Ave is split in half by the
El, so walk to the west side of the tracks before heading north.*

I have one nice thing to say about the Red Line Tap: the bottles of Pabst are cheap. Admittedly, my first visits to this Rogers Park bar were tainted by last season's meltdown of the Cubs, or more accurately, their fans. As the Florida Marlins hammered the New York Yankees, somber Cubs fans cried that their team belonged on the field, smashing the Yanks and winning it all. Customers jabbered on about the eighth inning of game six and cursed fan Steve Bartman. They groaned about a bobbled ground-ball, a wild pitch and a third out that was never meant to be. They were not unkind, just annoying, and baseball season could not end soon enough. Perhaps this was the wrong time to write about the Red Line Tap. I headed west and south, and waited for spring.

Spring brought hope, and North Siders, their team again stacked with talent, talked of happy things and once again dared to dream. I decided to give the Tap a second chance. Now, instead of whining like they had in the fall, the crowd was sedate. People said little. There wasn't a character in the place. It was just as bad as it had been in the fall, only more quietly.

Red Line Tap gets its name from the neighboring El line. The bar is new but the building is old, so Red Line Tap looks older than it is. Under a tin ceiling, men drink beer, down shots and talk about, well, nothing worth remembering. Gathered in back are tables, chairs, a small stage and people playing eight ball for beer. Customers scribble the walls with chalk—how cute—and up front, a cork board advertises local events and actors workshops. At the bar people read books under desk lamps (just ask the bartender for one). One couple brought in their bikes. I do not approve. The bar heats up on weekends (from cold to tepid) with live country, blue grass, or rock n' roll. (A band schedule is posted by the bathrooms.)

Some people apparently like the Red Line Tap. Some people watch NASCAR. I can explain neither.

Dive Rating: 1

NEAR NORTHWEST

BUCKTOWN, NOBLE SQUARE

RIVER WEST

UKRAINIAN VILLAGE

WICKER PARK

Club Foot

1824 W. Augusta Boulevard (Ukrainian Village)
773-489-0379

Hours: 8 p.m.–2 a.m., Sunday-Friday; 8 p.m.–3 a.m. Saturday
#50 Damen Ave. or #66 Chicago Ave. bus

Club Foot is half dive, half punk-rock cafe. The walls are decked out with photographs of the Buzzcocks, Iggy Pop and the Gang of Four. In glass cabinets you'll find kitschy figurines of characters like the Tick, Austin Powers, the Fab Four and Alfred E. Newman. Inflatables dangle from the ceiling. There's even an Ed Grimley lunchbox, outdone only by the signed Devo rain jackets. It's like drinking on eBay.

Indie punks populate the bar and bring with them the obligatory tattoos and piercings. The preferred manner of dress is jeans, wallet chain and an old T-shirt. Pin on small buttons and sew on a patch and you'll look like a regular.

The beer is cheap, yes, but I have a weak spot for the $2 well drinks. These cocktails are made with bad booze and lots of ice, but hey, two bucks is two bucks. Accompanying your booze is great punk, odd rock and those special songs that are so bad they're good. In back is a pool table and plywood boxes that are either tables or chairs. (Be careful you don't sit in a puddle of spilled beer.)

The men's room ranks high on my list of all-time greatest. The walls are papered in magazine pictures, a historical pop collage of the recent past. You could spend an hour in there just looking, rediscovering forgotten bands and remembering when rock idols where still young. The stall is dedicated to Elvis Presley, and a hundred Kings watch as you fill his porcelain throne.

Dive Rating: 4 ● ● ● ●

Club Foot

Ed and Jeans

Blue Line to Damen, then transfer to a northbound Damen #50 bus or
take a ten-minute stroll north

Do me a favor. Don't go to Ed and Jeans. Leave it be.

Ed and Jeans is an unspoiled, virgin dive. Located near a Tex-Mex restaurant and a pricey French bistro, it is a relic of a Bucktown that no longer exists. Jean runs the bar with her son, Larry. (Ed, Jean's husband, has passed away.) Jean is sweet and tough and can't see too well these days. When I presented my ID, she handed it to a regular, who then asked if he could borrow Jean's glasses. This same regular later beat me on the undersized pool table with one arm, and it was clear that I hadn't been the first: the rails were scarred from years of his running his cue upon them.

Later, that regular, a Kentuckian, mopped the floors and helped Jean close shop—at 10:45 p.m. on a Saturday. Jean said she doesn't usually keep her bar open that late, but the Sox were playing the Dodgers on the TV and L.A. had a 2–1 lead going into the ninth. Two strikeouts and a ground ball later, the bar officially closed.

It's a small place, about the size of a one-bedroom apartment. The walls are paneled with rec room–quality "wood" and covered with beer signs and Bears pennants. On a shelf above the back of the bar there's a diorama of a white Chicago Christmas, on display year-round. Miniature buildings formed from plastic grids laced with yarn sit on a blanket of cotton snow. One adorable row house is marked with Old Style insignia and a handwritten paper sign, the size of a cookie's fortune, that reads "Jeans."

The men's bathroom is very brown. The walls are wood paneled (again, like a rec room) and the ceiling light, soap dispenser and paper towel dispenser are uniformly stained with nicotine. Nailed to the wall above the toilet is a swatch of white shag carpet that always makes me think of cigarette filters.

The crowd? During a lull in the conversation with two pretty young women, one barfly sighed, relaxed his shoulders and said to no one in particular: "Oh boy, am I going to get bombed tonight." But not on cocktails. They won't make them. Besides, the bar has a poor selection and doesn't carry ice. Let me repeat that: the bar does not carry ice. So have an Old Style and a shot of bourbon for five bucks, and say yes when Jean asks if you want a glass.

God knows how long she will be doing this, but Jean told me to take some back issues of *Sports Illustrated* when I was leaving. There's a stack of them in the corner. She says they were her son's. If you're there one night and she offers, take one. It's the right thing to do.

Dive Rating: 9

Ed and Jeans

Gold Star Bar

1755 W. Division (Ukrainian Village)
773-227-8700
Hours: 4 p.m.–2 a.m., Monday-Friday; 3 p.m.–3 a.m.,
Saturday; 3 p.m.–2 a.m. Sunday
Blue Line to Division

NEAR NORTHWEST

The Gold Star Bar is a hip dive with a dirty past. In its speakeasy days, the Gold Star was rich, clean and comfortable. After the Second World War, the neighborhood deteriorated, and the bar started to come apart. Junkies, prostitutes and down and outs stayed in the flops upstairs, now apartments. Fights ended in homicides.

These days the scruffs hold art degrees, and the fights never get beyond a few huffy words. Some think, however, that the rough past still haunts the place. Phantasmic high heels have been heard clicking above, and psychic types get chills in the entranceway, where a stick-up man was once shot dead by a bartender. Lights turn off. Specters are there and then gone. Ironically, the bar is shaped like a question mark. At least one bartender says the spooks and rumors are rubbish, a sign some need to take it easy on the weed. A beefy man with a shaved head and goatee, he also refuses to believe he was once a professional wrestler. "I'm not a wrestler," he said. "Everybody asks me that. Even the guy at the video store. I should have told him I was, then decked a customer into one of the tape racks."

An Old Style costs $2 and Susan the bartender pours her shots dangerously deep. And I don't mind the free popcorn. But I do mind the plastic lawn chairs round the cocktail tables. At least they keep the yuppies out, as does the miserable raspberry paint and a stained couch that belongs in the alley.

Writing on the heating pipe in the men's toilet is a local obsession. Management frequently paints it over, but the enigmatic messages soon return. I found the following scribbled on the pipe on October 27, 2003:

Pipes Peak
Pipen Fresh
She's just not my pipe
Pipewriter
Piperback writer
Pipendicular
And now back by pipeular demand
Piper at the Gates of Dawn

CHICAGO'S BEST DIVE BARS

Scotty Pipen was never here
Stay off the pipe and don't forget to wipe
Pipey Long Stockings
The White Pipe
The Pipe of Greenwich Village
C'est ne pas un pipe

Dive Rating: 4 ⬤ ⬤ ⬤ ⬤

Gold Star Bar

The Beachwood Inn

1415 N. Wood Street (Wicker Park)
773-486-9806

*Hours: 4 p.m.–2 a.m., Monday-Friday; 3 p.m.–3 a.m.,
Saturday; 3 p.m.–2 a.m., Sunday (open at noon
Sunday during football season)
Blue Line to Damen*

If you look closely at the front door of the Beachwood Inn—named for the intersection of Beach Avenue and Wood Street—you'll notice a small hole at about chest height. That was where the bullet hit before burrowing into the bartender's arm. That was in 1973. According to the co-owner, Bob, the man shot the bartender because he asked him to move his stool down the bar in order to make room for a group. Tens years earlier, another bartender was shot, but he wasn't so lucky. Bob's father was killed in an armed robbery, leaving a widow with two boys to raise. Mom kept the bar. Now the boys run it.

The Beachwood is not violent these days. The toughs have moved out, replaced by the occasional condo owner and wearers of ironic used clothes, who in turn love the ironic '80s tunes on the jukebox. Fortunately, longtime neighborhood types still turn up for the $2.25 bottled beer specials. (Take note that the bartenders frown upon mixed drinks more complicated than a whiskey and soda.) There's also free food (chicken wings, pizza, etc.) on Sundays and Mondays.

Visit the Beachwood in the afternoon when there's still daylight to admire the collection of sports pennants (remember the Chicago Sting?) and tacky horror and rock-and-roll posters. The pool table is too ratty to warrant spending a buck, so I recommend the 25-cents-a-play Atari Millipede, my latest addiction. Beachwood also boasts a beautiful bar with wooden coolers, retro booths and a checkerboard floor.

Supposedly, a ghost lives in the basement and does harmless things like turn lights on and off. Some think the phantom is Bob's dad, but Bob is reluctant to believe. He doesn't like the thought of his father relegated to the basement. I agree. I'd much rather haunt the bar myself.

Dive Rating: 1

Gallery Cabaret

2020 N. Oakley (Bucktown)
773-489-5471

Hours: 5 p.m.–2 a.m., Sunday-Friday; 5 p.m.–3 a.m., Saturday
Blue Line to Western. There are, however, three Western stops on
the Blue Line. Exit at the North Side station, nearest O'Hare.

A few ill-chosen words at the Gallery Cabaret nearly got me into a street fight. A noisy rock trio had finished their set and were loading up their van outside. I passed the drummer as I left and offered him five bucks for music lessons. The band was soon after me. Thankfully a large acquaintance (who had played football for Notre Dame) helped calm the wiry rockers down.

Gallery Cabaret is an art dive, not a fight club, home to open mikes (wince), poetry readings (cringe) and drum circles (gag). One horrible night I had to witness all three, exposed to the artist collective SynchroniCity. SynchroniCity, from what I gather, exists to throw giant parties and burn things. Onstage a DJ played beats while members of the collective banged on drums. Some seized the microphone and free-styled badly. A video played, showing SynchroniCity members pounding drums and dancing around a giant bird of cloth and wood. Some held torches, others spun fire on the ends of ropes, a few spit flames from their mouths. They lit the bird and watched it roast.

"That was our first burn," a man next to me said. "It was in Wisconsin. At a biker bar."

I asked the man why he burned effigies and animal icons. I expected him to go on about ancient ceremonies, phoenix rising from the ashes, and the like. Instead he said, "I love burning stuff. Ever since I was a kid, I've liked bonfires. I grew up in the country, and we used to burn all sorts of shit out there."

Despite all its artistic trappings, the Gallery Cabaret isn't stuck up. Nobody minds the man sleeping on his stool or the cockroach that just marched the length of bar. The artwork on the walls isn't horrible and changes regularly. Beer is cheap enough. And if an artist collective ever torched the place, I'd grab that portrait of James Joyce before running for the door. I've always loved that thing.

Dive Rating: 6 ⬤ ⬤ ⬤ ⬤ ⬤

Inner Town Pub
1935 W. Thomas Street (Ukrainian Village)

Hours: 3 p.m.–2 a.m., Sunday-Friday; 3 p.m.–3 a.m., Saturday
Walking distance from the Blue Line's Damen and Division stops

You'll never grow tired of looking at the Inner Town Pub. Every shelf, corner and patch of wall is covered with something old, dusty and interesting. There are two large American flags—one with forty-eight stars and another made of advertisements from the Pepsi Free era—and plenty of smaller flags from across the globe. Elvis is honored in photograph, paint, porcelain and felt. A zoo of stuffed and mounted animals lives above the bar, and a Kennedy watches over the door.

Opened as the Inner Town Pub in 1983, the bar, under another name, is rumored to have once been a speakeasy. Tucked away in the Ukrainian Village, it has a quaintness that bars on busier streets (and that's most) lack, though the bar suffers frequent noise complaints from neighbors.

For me the Inner Town is too busy most nights, and it's packed Sunday and Thursday for the 10 p.m. open mike, one of the more popular in the city. Acts vary in talent but all performers earn one free beer. Drawbacks include a lousy sound system and a pool table that blocks the stage.

If you want peace and quiet, go during the afternoon when you can sip pints of Berghoff ($2.50) without getting elbowed by the crowd and listen to the gem of a jukebox.

The pool is free and far too serious. Pool rules are tacked to the wall to settle arguments. I've seen Mike, the irritable owner, explode and break up a game like it was grade school recess, screaming about how he'll take away the table. He is quite right. Wannabe sharks should take their sticks to a pool hall, not get pissy about slop on a beer-stained bar table. I last played a nasty old woman who haunts bars in the area, and is banned from some, and after I missed (an obvious shot, by the way) the hag referred me to the list of house rules, which is written on crinkled notebook paper. She read me the rule regarding the calling of bank shots. Then she tried to intimidate me. Right before she scratched on the eight.

Mike is a character. The gruff, old grump wears polyester and a frown, though talk to him as he checks IDs and you'll find him surprisingly nice. Mike's peculiar clothes betray a love for Elvis, and a good source swears he vacations in Florida in order to scuba dive and Jet Ski. One wonders if he removes those zip-up boots.

Dive Rating: 4 ⬤⬤⬤⬤

Inner Town Pub

Loop Tavern

Loop Tavern

1610 W. Chicago Avenue (Ukrainian Village)
312-226-6740
Hours: 7 a.m.–11 p.m., Monday-Thursday; 7 a.m.–midnight,
Friday & Saturday; 11 a.m.–7 p.m., Sunday
#9 Ashland or #66 Chicago bus

NEAR NORTHWEST

At Loop Tavern I've learned a few things about women.

"You've got to eat pussy," said one man, sipping Busch and selling socks. "Or be ready to lose your girl." Another agreed, then let me in on a little secret. "To test if a girl's clean, stick your finger in your ear then stick it in her pussy. If she cries 'Yowza!' she's dirty." Earwax was good for treating pimples, he said.

The language isn't always so crude at Loop Tavern, but don't expect fancy-talking society types. Expect the kind of men who argue over whose car is faster, or local street people who take a break from the cold with a beer and a discarded newspaper. The only woman I've seen at Loop Tavern was the bartender, a skinny, young Czech girl who wears shirts and sweaters that expose her midriff. Customers watch her more than Sports Center.

Loop Tavern has a liquor store up front, so you can leave with a bottle and some munchies. Signed softballs top the liquor shelves, and the cheap wood paneling has a lowbrow appeal. A bizarre ceiling consists of a hanging grid lit by long fluorescent tubes, which cause the bar to glow. The swill is Busch at $1.75 a can, but I've found the cocktails a better buy. A formidable Tanqueray and tonic costs $2.25, and a few ice cubes will struggle to keep it cool.

I'll assume the women's toilet is cleaner than the men's, where you'll be lucky to find toilet paper, paper towels or soap, but might spot a regurgitated burrito in the urinal.

Dive Rating: 7

Marie's Riptide Lounge

1745 W. Armitage (Bucktown)
773-278-7317

Hours: 8 p.m.–4 a.m., Sunday-Friday; 8 p.m.–5 a.m., Saturday
#9 Ashland or #73 Armitage bus

When I ask someone if they know a good dive, they first lament the clos-ing of Tuman's Alcohol Abuse Center, then ask if I've been to Marie's Riptide. Of course, I have. Who hasn't? This Bucktown lounge has been featured on *Late Night with Conan O'Brien* and *Crime Story,* Robbie Fulks and Michael McDermott have written songs about Marie's (don't worry: I've never heard of them either), and Marie's continually ends up on top-ten tavern lists.

Just not mine. Marie's Riptide has its charm and its champions, but it isn't the best dive in town. First off, bad beer costs four bucks. And the undersized, nothing-to-write-home-about cocktails cost five. Then there's the crowd. Before midnight, there's room and people are pleas-ant. After midnight, Marie's is ambushed by assholes. The bar has a four o'clock license, so when the local two o'clocks close, the thirsty head here. The crowd is hammered and trying to get laid, and you often have to line up to get in. At those late hours, the bar is terribly cramped, and the close quarters and general drunkenness lead to the occasional scuf-fle. Marie, who opened the bar in 1961, will intercede, bravely risking her old bones between dueling drunks. Of course, if Marie were hit, the crowd would tear the perpetrator apart.

Marie's does have its merits. The electronic skeet shoot is one of the great bar games. Its rudimentary screen hangs to the left of the door, and with the remote control, you can play from almost any seat at the bar. The décor is gloriously dated, with lots of linoleum and a fair share of tinsel. In the hot summer, the lounge is always extra cold, as if to brag of its air conditioning. The jukebox plays old 45s, to which Tina the bar-tender loves to sing along.

Marie's is not rough like it used to be. And there's nothing wrong with that. Neighborhoods change. But those that rank this bar top dive need to get out to the seedier sides of town.

Dive Rating: 3

Matchbox

770 N. Milwaukee Avenue (River West)
312-666-9292
Hours: 4 p.m.–2 a.m., Sunday-Friday; 4 p.m.–3 a.m., Saturday
Blue Line, exit at Chicago

When asked what kind of bar the Matchbox is, one bartender said: "This place isn't a dump, it's a dive. Once this guy called it a dump, and I threw him out." Matchbox bartenders will throw you out, and because there's no room to hide in this tiny, crowded, smoky cheesecake-shaped piece of heaven, you'll have to leave.

But try to stay. The Matchbox is my local and a bar with its own mayor. The booze selection is vast: twenty different brands of bourbon, twenty types of tequila, world-class vodkas and odd little liqueurs you've never heard of. It's a sophisticated dive, with cigars and imported cigarettes for sale. More than a bar, it's a place to get an education in drinking.

Some argue, even those in the very ranks of its customers, that the Matchbox is not a dive. No swill here, simply top shelf. A bit pricy. A fair share (and growing number) of suits. Did you say cee-gars? And, yes, they serve martinis.

But I give it the benefit of the doubt. On tap imports cost three bucks, and cocktails, though a bit steep at five, are professionally made with good ingredients. Tabs? Kept on cocktail napkins. Plus sticky counters, bar art and lippy bartenders. Sound like a dive now?

The Matchbox has no tables, and drinking is like riding a rush-hour bus. When you open the door, inevitably wedging someone against something very hard, cram aboard with sharpened elbows and stake a claim. As the crowd settles and inches towards the back to make space, throw up a hand, preferably with a little cash, and grab something for support. I prefer an old fashioned. Others go for the scrumptious whiskey sours, the famous margaritas or the deadly brandy Manhattans.

With drink in hand, don't be afraid to chat up one of the many people standing on your feet. The loss of personal space takes with it a good measure of inhibition, and those that don't engage in conversation tend to be good listeners. In such cramped quarters, they have no choice.

Dive Rating: 1

Phyllis's Musical Inn   1800 W. Division Street (Wicker Park)
773-486-9862

*Hours: 3 p.m.–2 a.m., Sunday-Friday; 3 p.m.–3 a.m., Saturday Blue Line
to Division and walk west*

Not far from this bar, at 1958 W. Evergreen Street, is a plaque com-
memorating Nelson Algren, who lived at that address for twenty-seven
years. However, Division Street is no longer the strip of gin joints that
Algren wrote about. Shots no longer cost a quarter, and you won't find
a poker game in back. The neighborhood has gentrified; the hustlers are
all but gone. Still, on a Sunday afternoon at Phyllis's Musical Inn, you
can catch a faint whiff of what it was like.

On the way to Phyllis's with a friend, I notice a man who doesn't look
before crossing the street. He wears many layers of old clothes to keep
out the cold and drags his feet, heels squashing the backs of his shoes
into slippers. We follow him into the bar. He joins his friends. Sun
shines through a wall of glass block. Dust floats through the light.

My friend and I order beers and the bartender asks if we are regulars. We
are not. She introduces herself, and we give her our names. "Now you're
regulars," she says. "Next round is on the house." A James Brown record
plays, and I look around. The bar is old, with wooden refrigerator cabinets and floorboards rubbed free of varnish. The brown tin ceiling has
corroded in parts. A wooden phone booth squats in the corner. It would
all make Algren proud.

I come back on a Wednesday night a few weeks later, and the crowd has
changed. Two young women dressed like Paris and Nicole prattle into
mobile phones. A woman asks for a credit card tab and is directed to an
ATM across the street. She returns and orders Raspberry Stoli and Coke.

Three bands are scheduled to play, and the first, a college duo, bugs the
bartender that they can't hook up the mikes. The busy bartender sends
a regular to fix the problem, and the duo soon takes the stage. They talk
too much and sing out of key. The crowd up front cheers them on. They
are friends of the musicians, or perhaps see them on campus. Above the
stage a mural of Chicago winds along the wall. Buildings dance around
an avenue of piano keys.

The older, wiser regulars gather at the bar's corner, by the door, as far from the stage as they can get. They suck down shots, snort, laugh and sneer. When the chirpy men on stage ruin "Rocky Raccoon," disgust boils over. Regulars let the insults fly. "You suck!" "Shut up!" "Someone flip the fuse box!" Paris and Nicole look back—as do others—but no one challenges the party in the corner. One regular approaches the band and insults them to their faces.

Later I play dice with a man who has been coming to Phyllis's for a decade. He tells me the bar will never change. "It will always be a neighborhood bar," he says. But tonight visitors outnumber him and his bunch, and Phyllis's is a good deal different from the taverns of The Man with the Golden Arm.

Dive Rating: 6 ⬤⬤⬤⬤⬤⬤

Phyllis's Musical Inn

Ola's Liquor

947 N. Damen Avenue (Ukrainian Village)
773-384-7250
*Hours: 7 a.m.–2 a.m., Monday-Friday; 7 a.m.–3 a.m.,
Saturday; 11 a.m.–2 a.m., Sunday*
#50 Damen Ave. bus. The Blue Line's Division station is a healthy walk away.

Rotten luck got me to Ola's. Once there I had a rotten time.

While I was driving down Lake Street to another dive, the hood of my car popped open and blocked the windscreen, and I nearly crashed into an iron El girder. With bent hood hinges I had to improvise, so I walked home, jumped on my bicycle and pedaled to nearby Ola's, a liquor store and bar in the Ukrainian Village. Outside hung an Old Style zimne piwo (Polish for cold beer), and to passersby, the front window presented a diorama of alcoholism.

I entered with little enthusiasm but perked up when I heard the bartender telling the two customers a story about her boyfriend. The tale ended with something like "and the cops never found the switchblade." With such a start, I thought the night promised lively banter. So I settled back with a ten-ounce glass of Pabst ($1) and waited for fireworks. Instead we watched television sitcoms and Blue Collar Comedy Tour: The Movie. The moron next to me felt compelled to repeat the redneck jokes, and he would later lead a heady conversation on what life would be like with three testicles. The resultant social isolation gave me much time to examine the room. Its few decorations included inflatable beer bottles, a portrait of JFK and a Where's Waldo map.

Ola's sells liquor to go, and when an indigent stopped in, he asked for the "cheapest bottle of anything." He was 19 cents short of a half-pint of vodka and treated rudely. A silent standoff took place between man and bartender as both sides waited for the missing change. To break the deadlock (the indigent was going nowhere), I feigned finding a quarter on the floor and gave it to the man, claiming he must have dropped it. I received no thanks for the coin, but the bartender gave me an ugly look. The bum left her a 6-cent tip.

Sometimes red-eyed yuppies slide into Ola's for just one more, but the regular set is of a more rugged cut. It's not dangerous, but I would only stop here again for a quickie and a six pack to go, though the $5 pitchers of Pabst remain a tempting reason to return.

Dive Rating: 7 ●●●●●●○

Richard's Bar

725 W. Grand Avenue (River West)
312-733-2251 or 312-421-4597
Hours: 8 a.m.–2 a.m., Monday-Friday; 8 a.m.–3 a.m.,
Saturday; 11 a.m.–6 p.m., Sunday
Blue Line to Grand

If the red, white and green awnings don't convince you that Richard's Bar is Italian, just go inside. You'll see photos of Italian actors, Italian ball players and a painting of Al Capone. A poster describes Chicago's most famous gang slayings.

The bar tunnels through the building on the corner of Milwaukee Avenue and Grand Avenue and can be reached from either street. The tavern is kinked, and on the short side is a small room with a couch. The long end contains the bar and take-away coolers lined with six-packs and 40-oz. bottles to go. Hardboiled eggs cost 75 cents.

Crowds vary. Late on a Saturday, I had to elbow my way through a mob to order a drink. I half expected a wet T-shirt contest to break out. On a weekday afternoon, I entered a hushed house of old men, quietly eating hot beef sandwiches, eyes glued to *The Pope of Greenwich Village.* A tough guy—a pressman at the *Tribune*—explained for hours all the fights he'd gotten in. On Sundays an old bartender approaches life—and violence—a bit differently, commenting on his old quarterback days. "I was stupid," he said, "but less stupid than the other guys on the team. When those tacklers broke the line and came down on me, I threw away the ball one way and took off in the opposite direction." He named the numerous streets the tacklers chased him down, as well as the many fences he had to jump.

I've heard the bar dates back to Prohibition and the building certainly looks old, but I couldn't get much out of Richard's tight-lipped bartenders. I suppose in time you could crack them, but I wouldn't call it time well spent. And who wants to wear cement shoes at the bottom of the lake.

Dive Rating: 5 ⬤⬤⬤⬤⬤

Rich's First One Today

2224 N. Leavitt Street (Bucktown)
773-235-9279

Hours: 11 a.m.–2 a.m., Sunday; 9 a.m.–2 a.m.,
Monday-Friday; 9 a.m.–3 a.m., Saturday
Blue Line to Western (the one closest to O'Hare)

Rich's First One Today, named after the owner's favorite toast, is a canine's paradise. You'll see all kinds of dogs here—Labs, golden retrievers, greyhounds—and a customer might rush home to get his pooch if he sees a similar breed scuttle through the door. According to the Chicago Department of Public Health, it is illegal to bring a pet into a restaurant or tavern unless it is a guide dog. So if Spot will be joining you for a drink, wear dark glasses. To the dogs' credit, they are exceptionally well behaved. The same can't always be said of the customers.

On a visit in the early evening, I found a fat-faced man who constantly bitched about everything and a glassy-eyed grandma who looked strung out on quaaludes and constantly nodded yes. A man with messy hair and dirt in the lines of his hands begged to be served another. The bartender agreed, but only if the man promised to shut up. He promised at considerable length, until once again told to shut up in the style of a Bugs Bunny gangster ("shut up shuttin' up . . . "). By 9 p.m. he had downed four more drinks and had been asked to shut up more times than that. Whole conversations had started and ended and started again, all on his inability to shut up. The bar decided it was time to for him to leave.

"Come on, just one more . . . " he started again. Soon everyone joined the fight to oust him.

"You've got a long drive back to the suburbs," one woman tried to reason with him.

"I'm asking you to leave because I care about you," the bartender said, pointing out that he had been drinking for four hours, and had promised upon his arrival that he would be out by nine o'clock. He argued, without looking at a watch, that it was not yet nine.

"Get the fuck out of here! Everybody wants you to leave!" one patron put it more bluntly. The drunk whimpered and then spoke one of those nonsensical lines that drunks say best. "What's wrong with everybody? You didn't treat me like this when I had a license and insurance."

When the old folks retire, the young came out to play. Rich's late crowd is the scruffy, twenty-something retro set. They dig the '70s and '80s songs on the jukebox, and I've caught a young man lauding Pink Floyd with a smirk. It could be worse. Being in one of the more secluded areas of trendy Bucktown has helped keep Rich's a cheap little secret. Pitchers of beer cost about $6, and the bartender will cook you a frozen pizza for $4.75. Go a few blocks east, and you'll be paying $5 for a pint and ordering focaccia. And that's just not the dive bar way.

Dive Rating: 5 ●●●●●

Dirty Dozen

Catcher's—*fightin' bar*
Domino—*Motherfucker!*
Ed & Jeans—*roach motel room*
Hangovers—*Chicago Vice*
Helen's Two Way Lounge—*two ways to leave, drunk or unconscious*
Lady Di's Pad—*scary, beautiful and scary*
Lemelle's—*if it's broke don't fix it*
The Marquis Room—*only for professionals*
Max's Place—*shut the door you're letting in light*
The Mutiny—*clean up your room*
Rothschild's Liquor Mart—*buzzer bathrooms*
Touché—*back room blowjobs*

Rothschild's Liquor Mart

1532 W. Chicago Avenue
(Noble Square)
312-421-1562
*Hours: 7 a.m.–10 p.m., Monday-Thursday; 7 a.m.–11 p.m.,
Friday and Saturday; 11 a.m.–7 p.m., Sunday*
#66 Chicago and #9 Ashland buses

Bad things happen when a bar is built in the back of a liquor store. Think bleach and toilet cleaner. Chili and Maalox. Leopold and Loeb. Frazier and Ali. The volatile mix at Rothschild's Liquor Mart on Chicago (there are several other Rothschild's in the city) is summed up by a sign on the wall that reminds patrons that fighting is not allowed. Another asks that you pay for your drinks when served and offers a $1 lottery ticket if the bartender fails to give you a receipt.

Despite Rothschild's double identity, booze bought up front at the store isn't allowed in back at the bar, so customers sometimes jump-start their evenings on the curb before returning inside and stumbling to a stool in the rear. Once at the orange Formica of the long, rectangular bar, patrons enjoy $5 pitchers of Bud or Miller. R&B blares on the stereo. The lights are tanning-bed bright and the island bar keeps customers facing one another. Everybody knows when you use the bathroom: the bartender has to buzz you in.

The clientele is rough. Once a man who looked like he slept in a doorway screamed at me three times: "If you dream you whoop me, you better wake up and apologize." These and other Ali bons mots helped his pool game, he said, pointing to a cramped table just feet from cue-scraped walls, by the dart board. Then there was the six-foot-five-inch hulk who told his cronies, as he strutted over to me and a friend, that he wanted to "show these white boys where they came from." He showed us many things, telling us about Shamballa, the city at the center of Earth; Queen Elizabeth II's blood relation to Satan; and how the movie Frankenstein was made to "help keep black people off the weed."

You'll drink fast at Rothschild's, because as soon as you get there you'll want to leave. Plus last call is 10 p.m., and soon after guys come out with brooms, sweeping cigarette butts onto your shoes as they slowly chase you and your pitcher around the bar. But you won't be herded out alone. On a Wednesday initiation to the back bar, I shook a few hands and shared many laughs, perhaps sensing each one may have been my last.

And though I wouldn't say I made lifelong friends, I do have the hulk's business card on my fridge. Will I call? When the sun shines in Shamballa.

Dive Rating: 10 ⦿⦿⦿⦿⦿⦿⦿⦿⦿⦿

Rothschild's Liquor Mart

Sak's Ukrainian Village Lounge & Restaurant

2301 W. Chicago Avenue (Ukrainian Village)
773-278-4445

Hours: 11:30 a.m.–2 a.m., Sunday-Friday; 11:30 a.m.–3 a.m., Saturday
#66 Chicago Avenue or #49 Western Avenue bus

Believe it or not, Ukrainians live in Ukrainian Village. Once a strong-hold of Eastern European immigrants, the Village now boasts more foreign cars than foreigners. But despite the growing number of condos and places to brunch, there's still a lot of old-fashioned flavor. Local landmarks include the National Ukrainian Museum, Holy Trinity Russian Cathedral and Sts. Volodymyr and Olha Ukrainian Catholic Parish. After you're thoroughly bored by these sobering stops, you can stuff your face and erase the memories at Sak's Ukrainian Village Restaurant & Lounge.

You'll find the restaurant airy and bright with lumpy booths and tables protected by plastic table clothes. Folk art covers the walls, and at Easter, cartoon bunny rabbits as well. The menu has some American food (burgers), but order something you can't pronounce. I picked a platter of Varenyky (Ukranian dumplings) stuffed with potatoes and sauerkraut and topped with sour cream and sautéed onions. The $11 feast included a bowl of borscht (beet soup) and a basket of bread. It was delicious and large, and by the time I downed the last dumpling, I was too stuffed for proper locomotion. My exit from the restaurant took a half hour and included a stop at a bar stool to catch my breath. The amused bartender asked what was wrong. I told her the cook was trying to kill me. She had filled my dumplings with cement. "Yes," the bartender said, "I should have warned you. Most people order just half a plate."

Another night I stuck to the lounge but had as much trouble exiting. It appears that the front door was designed for those who walk upright, and I found myself horizontal. I once again blame the bounty of Sak's, where every fourth drink is free. I wasn't told this until well into my fifth drink, and as a fiscally responsible barfly, I felt it my duty to capitalize on my investment and see myself to the second freebie.

Dive Rating: 3

Tuman's

2159 W. Chicago Avenue (Ukrainian Village)
773-782-1400

Hours: 3 p.m.–2 a.m., Monday-Friday; 11 a.m.–3 a.m.,
Saturday; 11 a.m.–2 a.m. Sunday
Don't ask me for directions. It's no dive, so find it yourself.

I once had a neighbor named Art, who restored old furniture he found in alleys. Trained at the Smithsonian, Art fixed blemished veneers with intricate, hand-cut patches of wood. But he would never take a restoration too far. On a prized chest of drawers with dazzling patterns of professionally stained wood, I noticed that one drawer was still covered in sloppy paint. Art kept this drawer unrestored to remind him of how the chest looked when he rescued it from the garbage.

Tuman's new owner lacks such sensibility. I've heard the new version with track lighting and flatscreen television is closer to the 1930s original, but I don't buy it. Sure the old gate, now cleaned and polished, is still up front, but the perch from the dirty couch is gone. And the new bar top is stunning, but it no longer holds up old rummies. An iPod has replaced the once great jukebox. I'm sure the yuppies who go to the new Tuman's love all the changes. I'm sure they love the wide selection of beers, the pretty cocktail waitresses and the kitchen in back. I'm sure they love the restored tin, the central air and the crystal clear sound system. And those huge tinted windows look efficient. Wow. Double paned.

Frankly it all makes me sick.

At the old Tuman's, the sign outside hung on hooks and swung dangerously on windy days. A registered Libertarian used to check IDs at the door. In the winter, customers would warm pot muffins on the hot radiators.

At the old Tuman's, you sat on torn stools or kegs of beer. The pool table in back was always busy, and the wretched bathrooms reeked of piss. A pint of Guinness was only $2.50. It's said the beer was so cheap because the owner had a deal with a distributor to get beer long past its sell date. At the new place, the beer is fresh and so are the lavatories. The pool table and the graffiti are gone. So is most of the character.

Tuman's Alcohol Abuse Center is dead. I've known this for a while, but it did not sink in. Not until I visited its replacement.

Dive Rating: 0

Zakopane Lounge

1734 W. Division Street (Wicker Park)
773-486-1559

Hours: 11 a.m.–2 p.m., Sunday; 7 a.m.–2 p.m.,
Monday-Friday; 7 a.m.–3 a.m., Saturday
Blue Line to Division. Look out for glass block windows and a colorful sign
that reads "Zakopane Little Town in the Mountain Maria's Lounge Ltd."

My suggestion is this: visit this Polish dive when the Polkaholics are playing. The fun and fast polka rockers are a laugh riot, with songs such as "Sauerkraut Is Sweet," "Dude Looks Like a Lady-hoo" and "May Miss a Note (but we never miss a party)." The trio performs in gold-sequined vests, gold bow ties and thick black glasses. Nerdy guitarist Dandy Don Hedeker, with his greasy hair, glasses and matted down and pronounced part, looked like a Hanson brother (Slap Shot) at the prom.

During a ballad honoring Old Style beer, the band drank out of 16-oz. Old Style cans kept cool in insulated cozies. At one point Hedeker addressed the crowd and said, "We may look like idiots. We may sound like idiots. But we've got our own website."

Polkaholic enthusiasm (and alcohol) inspired the crowd, who at first trickled then rushed to pack the space in front of the stage. They danced in pairs with sped up polka steps or spun wildly as one great mass. The chicken dance was a disturbing sight. Spurring them on was Cigar, an obnoxious, upstairs tenant who occasionally works at Zakopane, clearing up empty beer bottles. Cigar staggered around with a stogie in his mouth and two more sticking out from under his floppy cap. He played the fool and tried to get customers to dance. Also look out for Lil Wally, the Elvis Presley of polka, who plays here once or twice a year.

On nights without music—which are most—pool tables are pulled out and a curtain closes off the stage. For the most part people keep up front by the bar. After the Polkaholics finished, I realized this place wasn't for me, but, fortunately, Division Street left me with other options.

Dive Rating: 5

NEAR SOUTH

BRIDGEPORT
MCKINLEY PARK
SOUTH LOOP

Bernice & John's

3238 S. Halsted (Bridgeport)
312-326-9460

Hours: 3 p.m.–12 a.m., Monday-Wednesday; 3 p.m.–2 a.m., Thursday &
Friday; 11 a.m.–2 a.m., Saturday; 11 a.m.–12 a.m., Sunday
#8 Halsted St. bus

The South Side has something of an inferiority complex, much like Chicago's Second City syndrome. Southsiders detest North Side sophistication. Those up north usually disregard the South Side, which is by far the larger section of the city. When still new to Chicago, I asked a friend, born and raised in Logan Square, what there was to do on the South Side. "Nothing," he said. "Absolutely nothing."

Such pretentiousness is the best reason to head south. Up north on a Saturday night, good bars that dive during the week become overrun with dress shirts and hair gel. Women yap on cell phones, making, like, plans. Men high-five.

Bernice & John's could not be more different. Sure the crowd will mention, and often, that the Sox took the city series, but let down your guard and they'll buy you a drink. Make that several drinks.

Next-door to a Lithuanian restaurant and a storefront bursting with junk (its hand-written placard reads: Deconstructionist Art by Appointment), Bernice & John's inhabits a nondescript brick building with only a neon to hint there's a bar inside. The door to this Bridgeport tavern is kept locked. The barkeep buzzes you in. Mike, a bartender, said the buzzer keeps out the rough elements. It must work. The crowd inside is nice enough, though on my first visit, patrons were astonished to see a Northsider in their local. I asked a young woman how she knew I lived up north. "Your glasses," she said. Mine were made in Belgium. Hers were not.

The crowd stays civil with help from the swear jar. Customers must pay a quarter each time they use the "F word." Vulgarians are asked to leave. But it's mostly just fun. Every so often the swear jar is supposedly emptied, and customers are treated to free food. (I don't believe it for a second.) I fell in with a wily group of locals who bought me three shots and a beer (or was it two?) and invited me back to their place to wind the evening down. I returned the favor by buying them a round, and our thirsts, four plus the bartender, were satiated for $12. A bottle of Old Style, which my new Miller Lite–drinking friends considered beneath them, cost two and a quarter.

CHICAGO'S BEST DIVE BARS

The interior of Bernice & John's is by no means dramatic. The bar's top is Formica, the paint job green and white. Thursday night open mikes are on an itty-bitty stage in back. The jukebox carries a copious selection of rock 'n' roll. Various knickknacks add interest to the bar: old beer signs, a miniature traffic light that switches from green to yellow for last call (red closes) and photographs. Mike showed me one of him and his brother behind the bar as kids; he said they poured shots for customers before they could see over the counter.

Another sign of South Side wit and refinement hangs from the men's room door. It reads: Gentleman, please do not throw cigarette butts into the toilet. It makes them soggy and difficult to light.

Dive Rating: 6 ●●●●●●

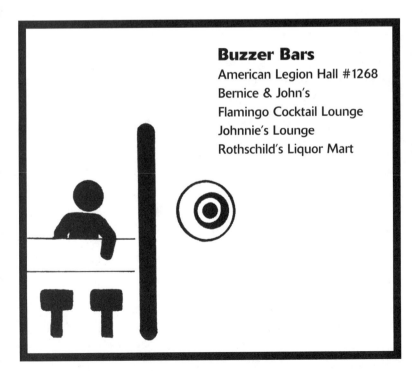

Buzzer Bars
American Legion Hall #1268
Bernice & John's
Flamingo Cocktail Lounge
Johnnie's Lounge
Rothschild's Liquor Mart

Catcher's

901 W. 35th Street (Bridgeport)
773-869-9411 or 773-376-4900
*Hours: 11 a.m.–2 a.m., Monday-Friday; 11 a.m.–3 a.m.,
Saturday; 11 a.m.–midnight, Sunday*
#8 Halsted bus

The note on the back bar read, "I, Pudge, am sorry for pissing in the men's room sink. I'll never do it again." The note was signed, "Pudge."

Catcher's, a Bridgeport sports bar near U.S. Cellular Field ("The Cell"), home of the White Sox, is unattractive. It is deep and dark and decorated with beer ads and televisions. The people are what make it pretty.

I was initiated on a cold Saturday night in April, after the White Sox dropped the second game of a double header against the Blue Jays. I had been driving east on 35th Street when I heard the last out on my car radio. Fireworks from the ballpark shot into the air. I stopped the car. To my right I saw Catcher's.

Sox fans packed the place, and I soon met Pudge, who wore a sailor's cap and leaned on the bar and grumbled. A small man with a white beard and leathery face, he looked like a garden gnome on a drinking binge. He mumbled something about karaoke. At Saturday karaoke tradition dictates that Pudge sings the first song, and a roar went up when he was announced. He sang My Way—the Pudge way—a style that slurs and requires heaps of profanity. The crowd loved it, and one man who yelled obscenities at Pudge soon felt the sting of a public teasing. "Hey, Jerry," a man said to the heckler. "Why don't you keep your general hatred for the world to yourself?"

Much beer was swallowed at Catcher's, and characters quickly came forward. A man who sang Rolling Stones in a bad British accent performed jazz leaps the length of the bar, his sister pirouetting behind him. While writing notes in the men's room stall, I overheard a mysterious transaction end with a man declaring, "God has given us too many pleasures."

My steward for the evening was a guidance counselor built like a longshoreman. He spent the time explaining how to knock a guy out. He said ever since he was a kid he had looked out for nerds like me. I asked him when his last fight was. "Last week," he said. Another fight seemed imminent, but the counselor's would-be opponent wisely backed down. I apologized to the man for the counselor's behavior, but he said don't worry about it, he'd changed his ways. "But a couple of years ago, we'd be out on the sidewalk right now."

Sox fans may fight (trust me, go to a half-price night at The Cell), but they know a good deal when they see one. Catcher's sells 16-oz. drafts for $1, a better price than at the Cubby Bear and the other yuppie bars clustered around Wrigley Field.

Dive Rating: 8 ●●●●●●●●

Eats

Billy Goat Tavern (Cheezborger!)

Cal's (Peppers Sandwich Shop)

Goal Post II (free soul food on select nights)

Sak's Ukrainian Village Lounge (Ukrainian)

Stadium West/Sue's Wok On Inn (Chinese)

T&T (Uncle Remus Chicken Shack)

Trojanek's Lounge (pizza)

Jack's Inn Between

733 W. 26th Street (Bridgeport)
312-225-7124

Hours: 11 a.m.–2 a.m., Sunday; 7 a.m.–2 a.m., Monday-Friday; 7 a.m.–3 a.m., Saturday
Orange Line to Halsted

I spotted Jack's Inn Between when I was returning from a visit to the Illinois Institute of Technology. I was with friends, and we had stopped at IIT to see some of its new architecture—Rem Koolhaas's El tube and student center and Helmut Jahn's student dorms—but something about the Inn Between's angled roof poking out between towering stacks of flats seemed more interesting than the sleek metal and tall windows of the new IIT additions.

As we entered, I was a little worried about Bing, a Chinese immigrant, receiving unwelcome attention from the locals. I should have worried about John and myself. As a man showed Bing how to play video slots, we were razzed as Northsiders and Cubs fans. "See that," one tough guy said, pointing to a White Sox pennant. "What do you think about that?" I dug into the Sox just enough to get a laugh and not a punch on the mouth. Soon we were all playing the free video bowling and talking about pro football. Yes, it's that kind of place, fully equipped with American flags and tributes to September 11.

More distinguishing are the little things. The Inn Between sells "P" Nuts and tiny packets of crackers and processed cheese. An LED sign lists upcoming events, informs that those caught using drugs in the bar will be prosecuted and congratulates a couple on the birth of a child. The shelves are carpeted—now that's different—and a corner display heralds the Emerald Society and Pipe Fitters Local 597, all over a statue of James Brown. Wine comes from both jug and box. If wine's too good for you, draft beer costs $1.25.

Duckie, the bartender, loves to decorate for the holidays. For Christmas, she writes regulars' names on little stockings; on St. Patrick's Day, on small shamrocks. I stopped in around Valentine's Day and found customers' names written on miniature hearts, pasted up behind the bar. The ceiling, though stained and sagging, was covered with red, pink, and white balloons. Cardboard covered the bathroom floor. Koolhaas, eat your heart out.

Dive Rating: 7 ● ● ● ● ● ●

3600 Club

3600 S. Damen Avenue (McKinley Park)
773-247-3939
Hours: 3 p.m.–2 a.m., Sunday-Friday; 3 p.m.–3 a.m., Saturday
Orange Line to 35/Archer

As far as bar reviews go, the 3600 Club had an off night. My first beer tasted stale. My pizza was not fresh. And I walked into the bathroom to find it flooding.

But I decided to give the 3600 Club some slack. The Newcastle tap was at the bottom of the barrel, and I visited late on Christmas Eve, when management on this Catholic side of town expects its customers to be at home or at Mass—not ordering pizza. The overflowing urinal? Just plain rotten luck (or dive bar gold?). As the night wore on, and the alcohol wore in, I started to like the place.

The large, wedge-shaped bar crowds the room, but you'll find people easygoing and talkative. If you bring a group, there are tables in back, and a personal pizza costs less than $6. Drinks are moderately priced. For the video slot addicts, there are three machines, though even in a scarcely populated bar, all three can be occupied for hours. For the interior decorator, there are mounted animal heads, a collection of Democratic whiskey decanters and a sign reading "Power to the South Side."

By the side door hangs a black-and-white photograph of the late Congressman John G. Fary, who originally owned Club 3600. Near the front door is an airbrush portrait of Mayor Richard J. Daley. In 1975 Daley anointed the sixty-four-year-old Fary as successor to Fifth District Representative John C. Kluczynski, who had died in office. An Internet search yielded little on Fary, aside from a column in the December 1975 Illinois Issue, which stated that shortly after Fary's induction into Congress, he fell asleep at the Capitol, "in full view of the visitors' gallery." Thankfully, the sleepy tavern owner and longtime politician didn't exit this world without leaving us his wisdom. On the back of the bar's business card is the following toast, found in the Congressman's memorabilia.

The wonderful love of a beautiful maid,
And the love of a staunch, true man,
And the love of a baby unafraid,
Have existed since life began.

But the greatest love . . . the love of loves,
Even greater than that of a mother,
Is the tender, passionate, infinite love
Of one drunken bum for another.

Dive Rating: 7 ●●●●●●●

Kaplan's Liquors

960 W. 31st Street (Bridgeport)

Hours: 11 a.m.–2 a.m., Sunday-Friday; 11 a.m.–3 a.m., Saturday
#8 Halsted bus to 31st Street

Officially called Kaplan's Liquors, this bar is known by the neighborhood as Marie's, after the owner. I'll always remember it for the moaner.

Kaplan's, or Marie's, or whatever you call it is like most liquor store bars—brightly lit, crammed with advertisements and seedy. Boxes are stored wherever there's space—along walls, under counters—and dirty floor mats are shredded to bits. Surveillance cameras record your every move. The digital jukebox suggests "DRINK MORE BEER." Shelves are packed with bric-a-brac such as model motorcycles and baseball batting helmets. A large ET doll sits in a Plexiglas case, and if you push a button, the alien's finger glows.

The female bartenders prefer stern expressions and are addicted to scratching lottery tickets. Occasionally they'll bring in some food, and I've had the luck to devour their homemade Korean vegetable pancakes. Miller ($1.25) is served in frozen mugs.

Regulars wear steel-tipped work boots, but on Mondays scruffy-haired hipsters migrate from up north to hang out with Ed, a bartender who writes and edits *Lumpen* magazine. As for characters, I've met a lady who named her son after an Elton John song and a Mexican who demanded I, then the bar, buy him beer. And there was the man with the moaner.

I had been sitting next to a man whose clothes proudly advertised his fondness for marijuana. Kaplan's was closing, and he asked me to join him for one last beer. He told me his house was just down the block. He seemed harmless. We arrived at his unfurnished home and he explained that he and a friend were remodeling it. Interesting, I said, but why was his friend lying semiconscious on the floor, wearing only underwear and moaning? My host insisted the man was sick, then asked if I'd spend the night. I declined, and it took some time to exit politely. We shook hands at the front door. He tried to grab me. I slipped his arms and ran to my car.

Dive Rating: 8 ⬤⬤⬤⬤⬤⬤⬤

Los Compadres Bar

3031 Archer Ave. (Bridgeport)

Hours: noon–2 a.m., Sunday-Friday; noon–3a.m., Saturday
Orange Line to Ashland

At Los Compadres Bar, the bouncer, who weighed 120 lbs. soaking wet, checked my ID then patted me down—my pockets, legs, the small of my back. He was checking for weapons.

"Do you find many guns?" I asked.

"No, I don't find many guns," he said. "Mostly knives."

Entrance to this ragged Mexican bar isn't always so difficult. Weapons checks are reserved for weekends, when the crowd dresses in their best cowboy hats and snakeskin boots. Most nights, the customers—mostly men—sit quietly at the bar, shoot pool or slap dominos at a table in back. Mariachi music blares, and beers are served with a lime cut into quarters and a shaker of salt. The bar counter, edged with red vinyl, pitches and leans and belongs in a west Texas cantina. The walls are plastered with posters of women in bikinis, but one more revered sits on the shelf behind the bar, a small shrine to Our Lady of Guadalupe.

My few experiences here include a serenade at my barstool and a strange scene one night after I left. I followed a man out to street and saw he had brought his beer with him (a sign on the door prohibits this). The man finished his beer then smashed the bottle in the street. He got into his truck—a bad idea—and pulled out to the middle of the road. There the truck stopped, the door opened, and out came a stream of urine.

Dve Rating: 9

Velvet Lounge

2128 1/2 S. Indiana Avenue (South Loop)
312-791-9050

Hours: 9 p.m.–2 a.m., Wednesday-Saturday; 8 p.m.–midnight, Sunday
#4 Michigan Avenue bus to Cermak Road and walk a block east

Of the world's many Velvet Lounges (a Google search turned up seven), I visited the nitty-gritty Chicago version on a night when the bank thermometers sported minus signs, the curbs were glazed with dirty snow and the Near South Side was desolate. As high-rise apartments shivered in the cold, an old brick building exuded the only warmth, housing a take-away rib joint with bullet-proof glass and a jazz club with caged windows.

Inside an old man charged $10 for admission. He is Fred Anderson, owner of the club since 1982 and a Chicago jazz legend. It was a slow night, and I later caught him napping at his post. The club can fill up quickly and one should arrive early, but on this cold night, only a third of the seats were occupied, mostly by University of Chicago students enrolled in a history of Chicago class.

My friend grabbed two seats and I went for beers ($3). When I leaned on the bar it moved, sloshing a customer's drink. Behind the bar were stacks of compact discs and cassettes. Photographs of musicians curled at their corners. On my side of the bar there were more photographs and enlarged articles about jazz musicians. One of soprano saxophonist Steve Lay was signed by the man himself. Beneath his name he wrote, "This place is a temple." In the back room a ragged looking stage faced a collection of wobbly cocktail tables. Red padded benches bordered the room, and black paint peeled from the ceiling.

I finished my beer and returned to the bar for another. The music started. A man seated near me told stories of musicians I had never heard of, while drinking from a glass of wine and a glass of beer at the same time. He told me, "Great musicians anticipate the future because they live on the edge." I nodded and walked back to my seat to listen to the set. Some of the students had fallen asleep, and others sat with crossed arms, eager to leave. When the quartet finished, the students rushed out to the awaiting school vans. One girl got left behind in the rush, so we gave her a ride home.

At 8 p.m. on Sundays, go see the Velvet Jam with saxophonist Dennis Winslett, percussionist Kobie Watkins, bassist Junius Paul and pianist Justin Dillard. They are joined by both local musicians and those passing through town.

Dive Rating: 7 ●●●●●●●

The Velvet Lounge

NORTH

GOOSE ISLAND

LAKE VIEW

LINCOLN PARK

LINCOLN SQUARE

OLD TOWN

RAVENSWOOD

ROSCOE VILLAGE

SHERIDAN PARK

Carol's Pub

4659 N. Clark Street (Sheridan Park)
773-334-2402

Hours: 9 a.m.–2 a.m., Monday-Tuesday; 11 a.m.–4 a.m.,
Wednesday-Friday; 11 a.m.–5 a.m., Saturday
Red Line to Wilson

Chicago's closest thing to a honky-tonk, Carol's Pub has a dank and depressing reputation it doesn't quite deserve. Or rather, I've seen worse.

I stopped by on a Saturday to find the bar packed with college grads who stomped like it was an Intro to Dance outing. Led by the house band Diamondback, who strummed country covers and took requests for dollar bills (though they looked a little weary of the same old scene, same old songs), the raucous, corn-fed crowd sat at long tables crowded with Miller Lite empties. Each additional round sent another couple to the dance floor to two-step. A few of the dancers were quite good. Others made up for poor skills with embarrassing enthusiasm. Seedier types roamed the fringes or sat at the curvy bar. I stuck with them and drank a lousy Busch for $2.50. A sign offering $4 pitchers of Bud on Monday—two days away—greatly irked me.

As expected in a joint with a rebel flag on the wall, the customers are mostly white. Ladies pack Carol's on weekends. Weeknights are far less busy, with the daily drinkers jabbering and stuffing dollars in the jukebox. Thursday karaoke brings all sorts. Hamburgers, chicken and shrimp are available from the grill. Eat at your own risk. A pool table is squeezed into a room in back.

Perhaps times have changed. This neighborhood has cleaned up, so maybe old stories of hillbilly beer brawls and prostitutes are true, though things seem relatively tame these days.

Dive Rating: 4 ●●●●

CHICAGO'S BEST DIVE BARS

Carol's Pub

Crabbby Kim's

Crabbby Kim's

3655 N. Western Avenue (Roscoe Village)
773-404-8156

Hours: 11 a.m.–2 a.m., Monday-Friday; 11 a.m.–3 p.m.,
Saturday; Sunday, 11 a.m.–midnight
#49 Western Ave. or the #152 Addison St. bus

NORTH

Call me a dreamer, but I have long been waiting for a bar that fills the gap between Hooters and a full-fledged strip club. A place without covers and with reasonable drink prices, where I could go see more than just a stuffed T-shirt but not be asked every three minutes if I want a lap dance. Crabbby Kim's was supposed to fill this slot, but falls way short. It's just a sports bar with a little bit of skin.

Gentlemen, you'll never get laid here, as the clientele is mostly local males, some sporting the odd NASCAR jacket or baseball cap mullet. The entertainment consists of listening to bad music, drinking Miller Lite and ogling the bartender. If you're lucky, she might caress a nipple or give her breasts a shake. A regular told me that about once a year a lady loses her top.

Still, it beats Hooters, which is not saying much. No birthday songs. No $20 Buffalo wings. Kim's serves a good 1/2-lb. hamburger with fries at a great price, $2, on Sunday and Thursday. Plus you don't have to drive to the mall to get there, then sit next to obnoxious executives in golf shirts.

Crabbby Kim's half-hearted attempt at a Jimmy Buffet/surf shack motif includes a half dozen surfboards advertising beer brands, more neon beer signs than are worth counting and a giant inflatable bottle of Corona. There are posters with bikini-clad beauties rolling around on the beach, longing for a cold one. I think my mechanic has the same ones.

I had high hopes when I heard of this bar. I envisioned bartenders flashing tits for tips, tall Cinderella shoes and the occasional bar dance. I imagined a joint where I could stop in for a peek and not blow my wad. I would have settled for saggy boobs, bad lighting and the leering of old men. But, it ain't all bad. The ladies behind the bar are pleasing to tired eyes, as the black lights nicely accentuates their attributes and those dainty little bikini strings. And when the bartender turns her back to the customers, watch as all eyes drop to her fanny. Then take a good look yourself. Don't worry. No one's going to tell.

Dive Rating: 3

The Hideout

1354 W. Wabansia Avenue (Goose Island)
773-227-4433
Hours: 8 p.m.–2 a.m., Monday; 4 p.m.–2 a.m.,
Tuesday-Friday; 7 p.m.–3 a.m., Saturday
Parking is plentiful, or take the nearby #72 North Ave bus

Well hidden, well known and well loved, the Hideout is a tiptop tap.

Wedged between warehouses, the Hideout officially started slinging drinks in 1934 (wink, wink), just after Prohibition ended. The bar catered to workers from local factories, opening early, closing in the evenings and shutting down on weekends. A back room was added in the 1940s, with a restaurant that served breakfast, lunch and dinner. With no houses nearby, factories kept the bar running.

These days the bar stays open late and is considerably less proletarian, home to more working artists than working stiffs. One bartender is a poet. A doorman, when not checking IDs, composes music in his notebook. For fun, the staff put together an album. Patrons discuss socialism and art. Prices are cheap, and the dress code is as you are.

The place is gorgeous. In the front room, old beams bend beneath a sagging ceiling of old tin, painted gold. There's a glorious absence of advertising, aside from tasteful band posters and announcements for upcoming events. In a shrine near the men's room, a candle lights a painting of a holy woman dressed in tight pants, biker hat and jeweled black brassiere. She stands with her arms hanging, flames burning behind her. Elsewhere a glass case displays thick old beer cans with pull-tab tops.

The back room more than doubles the bar's size and includes a stage. Mounted swordfish and muskellunge curl off handsome wood paneled walls, and strings of lights dangle from exposed studs. A small bar in the back serves beer when the house is packed, and supports turntables when needed. Blue grass, blues, pop, jazz, country and folk bands play here, and I've even heard accordion rock. DJ dance parties, short films and improv also appear on the menu. A piano waits in the corner.

Of the four owners, Tim Tuten is the most noticeable. He's the curly headed neurotic who delivers long, heartfelt monologues before the Hideout's more popular shows. Before he bought the bar with his wife, they used to drink here, as did his dad. If this bar has a heart it's him.

The Hideout can be deserted on a Saturday or packed to the gills in the middle of the week. There's usually no cover, but donations are encouraged.

Dive Rating: 2 ⬤ ⬤

The Hideout

Carola's Hansa Clipper

4659 N. Lincoln Avenue (Lincoln Square)
773-878-3662

Hours: 10 a.m.–2 p.m., Sunday-Friday; 10 a.m.–3 a.m., Saturday
Brown Line to Western. The #49 Western Avenue and #11 Lincoln Avenue.

I first heard of Carola's Hansa Clipper from a co-worker. She reported seeing a man at the bar carrying a sword. And rumor had it that the old flag above the pool table was a Nazi banner that once flew over occupied France. The rumor is not true. The flag, which bears a black eagle at its center and an iron cross in the upper left corner, dates from before the First World War. Though I've yet to see swords, I've seen several sharp mullets. I have also heard Bach play peacefully on the stereo and know sweet ambrosia flows from the taps.

The bar sits in sedate Lincoln Square, on a stretch of Lincoln Avenue that feels like a small town. If not for the bay windows, one might confuse the Hansa Clipper with a converted suburban basement. Maps and photographs of Germany are tacked to the walls, and above the register hangs a homely woodcut sign that reads "whatucezwhatugit." A mounted animal head or two and the odd snapshot collection complete the picture.

The crowd is pleasant and corny and may say "Auf wiedersehen" when you leave. But don't think they lack spark. On my last visit, a handsome old Austrian in a suit coat said to me about an enemy at the bar: "I fucking smash his face in. I just want to have a little fun. He come over here, and I smash his face open." The two men had been trading empty threats all evening, the Austrian occasionally hissing like a devil. A woman who could lick them both kept them apart; the bartender let them carry on. She obviously had some experience with the two, as she continued to serve them.

Between outbreaks, the hissing Austrian would stumble over to me and my lady friend to apologize for his unruly behavior. Arms around us, he'd rock on his heels and explain his side of things, then demand loudly to buy our next round. He soon lost track; the bartender did not. I had three large mugs of beer before I paid again; my partner, four vodka tonics without dropping a buck. Later I caught the Austrian mumbling to himself, "I'm going to be in big trouble in the morning."

Dive Rating: 3

Friar Tuck

3010 N. Broadway Street (Lake View)
773-327-5101

Hours: 2 p.m.–2 a.m., Monday-Friday; 2 p.m.–3 a.m.,
Saturday; noon–2 a.m., Sunday
Brown or Purple Line to Diversey and walk east

With few dives left in this safe, affluent and pretty part of town, populated by lovers of Friends, Friar Tuck is as rugged as it gets. Opened in 1970 by Angelo and Christine Como, the bar is still family owned and operated. Mrs. Como, who no doubt prefers Christine, was friendly. She introduced me to my bar-mates and later coaxed a woman suffering a cold into sipping a snifter of hot apricot brandy.

From the outside this beer barrel–shaped bar looks intriguing. Inside it looks like a frat party, though I find no fault with the $4.50 mini-pitchers. The bar is a dungeon of dark, soothing wood. A copper fireplace blazes in winter. The ceramic-topped bar with copper trough is cute and a bit crooked. Customers crunch free popcorn and hail old friends. Darts are played in back. It would help if the boring snapshot collections of partying patrons and the numerous gaudy advertisements were ripped down.

Rounds are tabulated on an old mechanical cash register, but tunes blare on a loud, newfangled jukebox that makes conversation a chore. From a big book of songs, customers request tracks that can be downloaded to the box once a week. Popular songs remain in the jukebox's memory. The unpopular are replaced. On my watch, jukebox democracy at Friar Tuck led to repeats of U2's "With or Without You" and Van Halen's "Hot for Teacher" within a half-hour time frame. Unacceptable. A benevolent dictator/DJ needs to seize control.

Dive Rating: 1

Hungry Brain

2319 W. Belmont Avenue (Lake View)
773-935-2118

Hours: 8 p.m.–2 a.m, Sunday, Tuesday-Friday; 8 p.m.–3 a.m., Saturday
#49 Western Ave. or #77 Belmont Ave. buses

NORTH

Retro, clean and stylish, Hungry Brain hangs dangerously on the cusp of pseudo-dive. But the Brain just makes the cut, helped by its classic façade faced with white, lunch tray–sized squares, the kind seen on old Texaco stations. A lone Leinenkugel sign blazes in front, and the front window elegantly curves. Hours are written on a note card in the window.

Enter the Brain and you're suddenly backstage, wondering if this is the right address. To your right is a row of wooden theater chairs, and velvet curtains dangle to stage level, blocking off the main room. The stage hails from the building's past life, when it housed an improv comedy theater. (The building had two more floors that were destroyed by fire.) Improv still plays on Wednesday nights, jazz on Sundays. Follow the black corridor to the bar and you'll find a tavern of impeccable taste. The ceiling is painted periwinkle, the walls a washed-out yellow. Besides exhibited art, you'll be hard pressed to find anything new here, among the ratty booths and old cocktail tables with marble tops. Much of the furniture has been donated by friends or found in alleys. Huge ashtrays are shaped like prehistoric fossils, and streamlined lamps are a thrift-store score.

CHICAGO'S BEST DIVE BARS

Janis and Luz, the owners, opened Hungry Brain in 1997, and named their bar after a club in the Jerry Lewis movie *Visit to a Small Planet.* A small movie poster is framed behind the bar. Also back there is a collection of brains, including a rubber one hooked by tube to a Jägermeister IV.

There is much to like about Hungry Brain: the $1.75 Pabst Blue Ribbon, the Kinks on the jukebox and an Arkanoid you can play while waiting for the bathroom. But if the Brain has a drawback, it's the crowd. They come in groups and stay in groups. On the flip side, the Brain is a fine place to be left the hell alone. For those looking to be underwhelmed, rumor has is it that the Brain's piano once belonged to Liberace's piano tuner.

Dive Rating: 1

Lincoln Square Lanes

4874 N. Lincoln Avenue
(Lincoln Square)
773-561-8191
Hours: noon–2 a.m., Sunday-Friday; noon–3 a.m., Saturday
Brown Line to Western

Lincoln Square Lanes sits atop a hardware store, and on weekends throngs of pretty people dressed in jeans laugh as they roll balls into the gutters. And who can blame them for laughing. The alleys look like such fun, with old equipment that lacks Big Lebowski luster but exhibits a homely charm—no electronic scoring. Above the lanes is a mural painted in three-point perspective that looks half fantasy art, half Atari 1600. Lincoln himself sits pensively at its center. Towards him rolls a white ceiling, like a set of waves seen from beneath. A balcony with lockers looks over the twelve lanes. Open bowling costs $3 a game, and shoes rentals are $2. Call to make sure a league hasn't booked the lanes, though they usually end their tournaments before 10 p.m.

For non-bowlers, there are video slots and pinball. A long counter and windows let you sit and watch alley action from the lounge. The clientele includes a good helping of women, a rarity at dives, though few hang out at the bar. The jukebox plays a lot of Def Leppard.

Dive Rating: 1

L & L Tavern

Hours: 11 a.m.–2 a.m., Sunday-Friday; 11 a.m.–3 a.m., Saturday
Red, Brown or Purple Line to Belmont and walk east

NORTH

Once upon a time, Lakeview was cool, but now all that's left is the L & L. And even that has changed. Julian, a longtime customer, a part-time employee, a stage actor and one of the world's great cigarette bummers, said when he first started coming here, the L & L was a full-blown dive. From there it went to actor's bar. Now it's "eclectic." Still, Julian calls it a magical place, and I'll stick by him.

You'll find a fair amount of wannabe punks here, including some of the white belt and jeans set, but what's important is that the drinks are still cheap and the bartenders still ornery. They have whiskey specials. The last one I had was Merrys Irish Whiskey for $2.50. Wicked stuff, and Pabst Blue Ribbon and Huber Bock still cost a refreshing $2.

The décor is dirty and green. A bartender said the place has been a bar, under various names, since 1934, and that its current name comes from two former owners, Lucky and Loretta. The jukebox is excellent. It's turned up loud and must be the only one in the country with an album by the Tindersticks. Tables and chairs are scattered about, and no one much minds if you fall asleep in the corner.

CHICAGO'S BEST DIVE BARS

L & L is renowned for its "absinthe." Illegal for sale in the United States, the strong herbal liqueur has a fabled history and supposedly produces a mild psychedelic experience similar to that produced by smoking weed. The L & L's version combines absente ($6) with wormwood ($6), poured over a sugar cube. That the two are not produced together supposedly makes the L & L's concoction legit. Research absinthe, however, and you'll find it is not made so easily, so one should be skeptical of this Chicago recipe. To be fair, the L & L makes no wild claims about its brew, which tastes like a very bitter pastis. Still, it's fun to try, and worth pissing off a bartender when you ask for it.

Dive Rating: 4 ● ● ● ●

L & L Tavern

Johnnie's Lounge

3425 N. Lincoln Avenue (Ravenswood)
773-248-3000
Hours: 9 p.m.–2 a.m., Sunday-Friday; 9 p.m.–3 a.m., Saturday
Brown Line to Paulina

Few stop at Johnnie's Lounge, a Lincoln Avenue relic whose days are numbered. Those out and about in trendy Ravenswood prefer bars with names like Fizz, J. T. Collins and the Lucky Strike. Loiter outside and you can watch these pretty people click by in dress shoes and $100 jeans. Note the shimmer of their hair and the shrillness of their "oh-my-god"s. Johnnie's just isn't their kind of bar.

But for barflies this lounge is a welcome fix on a side of town where dives are dropping from the map. To us, Johnnie's faded Hamm's beer sign shines like a beacon. And the muddy lot with its two old caravans feels truer than any beer garden. It's here that John, the owner, sells pumpkins in the fall and Christmas trees in December.

In thirty-five years, John has been the place's only bartender. He came to Chicago from Yugoslavia in 1957, and when he opened the bar twelve years later, he was working as a machinist by day and a bartender by night. He is retired now, which means he only works seven nights a week. He has never returned to Europe, claiming he was always too busy.

The door to the bar is always locked. To enter, tap on the window until John buzzes you in. Inside you'll find a kinked cave draped in cheap wood paneling. The bar used to be a flower shop before John took over, and little seems to have been added since. The tables are hedged in by meticulously placed chairs. My guess is they rarely move. Rows of bottles and glasses age under a coat of dust. The only modern touch is a color television placed awkwardly in the corner, too far from the bar. Johnnie's is actually quite big, and its emptiness makes it seem even bigger.

On a Saturday night, it may be just you, John and *Hollywood Squares.* On top of the pool table are opened envelopes and John's reading glasses. One can hear the radiator ticking. Lonely ashtrays line the bar, each furnished with a faded pack of matches.

John says he somehow, but barely, renews his liquor license each year and hints that his doors may soon shut forever. It's time for him to retire for real. Visit while you can.

Dive Rating: 8 ⚫⚫⚫⚫⚫⚫⚫⚪

Max's Place

4621 N. Clark Street (Sheridan Park)
773-784-3864
Hours: 7 a.m.–2 a.m., Monday-Friday; 7 a.m.–3 a.m.,
Saturday; 11 a.m.–2 a.m., Sunday
Red Line, exit to Wilson

Max's exterior sign reads: Where Friends Meet Friends. A more honest motto might read: Where Lonely, Washed-Up Old Men Come to Drown Their Sorrows in Suds. This ugly little dump is an absolutely wretched place to spend an evening.

I first visited Max's the night before Thanksgiving, numbing my brain for the inevitable torture the next day would bring. Not a soul spoke to me, besides a drunk Mexican who slurred on and on, in very broken English, about an empty barstool. The only other action was a gap-toothed, Joe Piscopo look-alike in sweatpants dancing to "Night Moves."

A believer in second chances, I tried Max's again. My first encounter was with a man wearing tight braids who sold used books at Canal Street on Sundays (a great place to fence), where an all-season bazaar has replaced the Maxwell Street Market. He tried to sell me a book. I didn't want a book. He reached into his bag for another item, but I refused before he could fish anything out. Then he tried to sell me the bag.

At the end of the bar sat three Sioux Indians, one sleeping forehead to the bar, a Stallone movie on the TV above. When Sleepy woke, the first thing he said was "Get me a beer!" Then Sleepy's son, a real asshole from New York, showed up, along with his son, a real asshole from Texas. The New Yorker tried to bully everybody in the bar, and his Texas son barked at me to slide down a stool. I refused until asked politely. He sat next to me and asked what I was drinking.

"Old Style," I said.

"Old Style? That's fucking shit," he said, taking a smug swig from his Bud Lite. He then commanded the bartender to, "Get this guy a beer." I refused. You don't want to be indebted to people like this.

Dive Rating: 8 ●●●●●●●●

Old Town Ale House

219 W. North Avenue (Old Town)
312-944-7020

Hours: noon–4 a.m., Sunday through Friday; noon–5 a.m., Saturday
Brown Line to Sedgwick

This brown, smoky den dubs itself "Chicago's Premiere Dive Bar," yet sits in a neighborhood dominated by yuppies. A movie theater and shopping complex loom across the street. Overpriced antique stores and trendy restaurants are right round the corner. Sadly, the Ale House remains the only throwback to the Old Town that once was.

The original Ale House opened across the street in 1958, but a fire forced a move to the current address, a former German butcher shop. The railed-in area at the back, now a pen for a pinball machine, video games and shelves of books, used to be the store's counter. Sausages once hung in the front windows.

Regulars have played a big part in the history of this bar, and a mural from the early '70s caricatures the barflies of that era. Today's regulars are immortalized by painter Bruce Elliot, whose framed portraits pack the south end of the bar. Try to match portraits with the faces in the crowd. Famous Ale House customers, many of whom worked at the Second City theater, include comedians George Wendt and Rob Schneider. Brian Dennehy has visited enough to earn an Elliot portrait, and Chris Farley tipped a few back the night before he died. Before Star Wars, Harrison Ford did carpentry work on the bar.

I have heard a story about two Blues Brothers buffs who stopped in to photograph the barstools where John Belushi and Dan Ackroyd once sat. Told that the stools had long been replaced, they headed toward the door, disheartened. "Get back here," the bartender called to them. "If you want a photograph, go to the bathroom. The urinal was never replaced." They went in and snapped away, happy to document where the Blues Brothers once pissed.

Fame is one thing, but I go to the Ale House for the regulars, all of whom seem to have nicknames (e.g., Carpenter Pat, English Dave and CIA Bill, who told me, "Don't believe them: I'm not really CIA."). I also go for the stubbornness: the jukebox refuses to play rock 'n' roll, and the customers, with whom I frequently argue, refuse to accept I'm right.

Dive Rating: 5 ●●●●●

Old Town Ale House

Rose's Lounge

Hours: Closes at 2 a.m. #11 Lincoln Ave. bus or take the Brown or Purple Line to Diversey

On a Tuesday night at Rose's Lounge an old man went to the bathroom and returned to find that a young, attractive woman had taken his chair. (Well, one of his chairs: he occupied several.) Instead of pulling up another stool, he cursed the woman, angrily pointing out proper bar etiquette: "My beer is here, my jacket there—of course, it's my fucking chair." As he grumbled on, the bartender threatened to telephone Mom, a.k.a. Rose, the bar's owner. It seems that Rose had recently lectured the temperamental customer about his outbursts. The man denied ever being told off. The bartender dialed Rose. The man shut up.

Rose is central to the life of Rose's Lounge, a small, dive lover's oasis in upscale Lake View. She's asked about when not there, and when she saddles up behind the taps, even newcomers address Rose as if they've known her a lifetime.

Rose is, of course, a piece of work. In the midst of friendly conversation, she pinned World War II on Jesse Owens, saying his gold medals at the 1936 Olympics so enraged Hitler that he tried to conquer Europe. One man, in for a game of pool and a nightcap, made the mistake of asking Rose when the lounge closed. She regarded him with a cold stare and, when he left, complained to the bar, "Who does that jerk think he is? This is my bar. We close when I say we close."

Rose's is often besieged by students—Depaul University is just south—but still buzzes with its own line-up of barflies. Visit a few times in a week, and the flies will swarm to you. Rose manages the introductions and caters the affair with $1 drafts and free pretzels.

The decorations are those typical of dives: a bust of Elvis, a collection of china plates, cups and figurines and an old photograph of downtown Chicago. A few potted plants do the place wonders, and a framed picture of a Hawaiian beach makes it feel as if the surf and sand is right outside the front door. (It actually doesn't feel that way at all.) The superb jukebox only accepts quarters and plays old 45s, including a wonderful and worn out "(Sittin' On) The Dock of the Bay." For fun you can peak through the glass and watch the mechanical arm load the records.

Dive Rating: 6

Rose's Lounge

Shoes Pub

1134 W. Armitage Avenue (Lincoln Park)
773-871-4640

*Hours: 11 a.m.–2 a.m., Monday-Friday; 11 a.m.–3 a.m.,
Saturday, noon–2 a.m., Sunday*
Brown Line to Armitage

Shoes Pub will soon walk no more. As of publication, it has about eight months left to live, according to Karen, the bar's bartender and manager. She says Frank, the owner of Shoes and the nearby Burgundy Inn, is getting on in years and no longer wants to run Shoes. Plenty of people would like to keep the bar going, but Frank's license is in his name and won't transfer. Why doesn't someone apply for his own license, then? Since being elected in 1989, five-term Mayor Daley has clamped down on city taverns, closing bars and making it hard to get tavern licenses. As a result, about half as many taverns exist today as a decade ago. In a July 2003 article in *Chicago Magazine*, a North Side alderman said it best: "If someone came in here wanting to get a tavern license, I'd pretty much let them know right up front that the answer is no. We haven't done a tavern license in a long time."

Yet for Shoes even this might not matter: the lease is also a problem. Owners of the building have indicated that they will not renew. Karen speculated that they'll turn the building into condos. And yuppies don't want a noisy bar downstairs.

Oddly enough, I took notes on this bar on a night it was honoring the dead. A regular had passed away and his drinking buddies had gathered to celebrate his life. Karen, in her fishbowl glasses and I'm-Not-Deaf-I'm-Ignoring-You T-shirt, gave out free Old Style, the deceased's staple drink. Burgundy Inn supplied the pizza. The mood was festive, and I flirted with two women who took turns cracking nuts. Later we played a game of darts. A serious darts bar, Shoes has very nice equipment, though the set-up of the bristle boards takes getting used to. (Dartboards are kept in lit plywood boxes that make them seem closer than they actually are.) Shoes sells darts equipment in a store the size of a broom closet.

Named after the long defunct disco Dancing Shoes, the bar is home to what one patron called "carpenters, tradesmen and working class stiffs." Drinks are cheap, and the daily special—a 22-oz. Rolling Rock for $2.25— will keep budget drunks well lubricated. At least for eight more months.

CHICAGO'S BEST DIVE BARS

Dive Rating: 3 ●●●

Town Hall Pub

3340 N. Halsted Avenue (Lake View)
773-472-4405

Hours: 11 a.m.–2 a.m., Tuesday-Friday; 11 a.m.–3 a.m., Saturday
Brown, Purple or Red Line to Belmont and walk east to Halsted Ave.

The queerest thing about the Town Hall Pub isn't that it's a straight bar in Boystown, ground zero of gay Chicago, but that it's a Grateful Dead bar. And, mindful of its dirty little secret, the Pub doesn't want to be outed. In a neighborhood with window displays pushing leather undergarments and street corners marked with rainbow-ringed monoliths, Town Hall Pub is quietly announced by an inconspicuous green awning. Without an exact address, I would have never found it, and when I first ducked in, I encountered an unmanned counter and racks of booze to go. For future summer afternoons I noted that the pints of whiskey, vodka, gin and tequila were perfect for smuggling into nearby Wrigley Field. Behind the to-go room is the narrow main room and bar.

Having seen firsthand what Grateful Dead music can do to a person's cleanliness, I had low expectations for the Pub. I pictured ashtrays choked with butts, an odor of incense and bong water, alleyway furniture and a shirtless man with blonde dreadlocks handing out grilled cheese sandwiches. But besides the stained ceiling that dripped water into a puddle behind my stool, Town Hall was spotless.

The bar counter is great. Through its murky clear-coat finish, one can see odd drawings and magazine cutouts. And across it pass top-notch drinks. Warsteiner in cans was on special for $2, but I tried the bartender's hand at cocktails. He made a fine rum ricky, served in a sturdy old-fashioned glass, and his potent, three-shot margarita ($6) impressed. Specials vary, but there's always a selection of $1-shots. The hideous list includes Raspberry Pucker, Jello shots and root beer schnapps.

The crowd was more starched than I expected. At one table sat four men in dress shirts. But there was a bead here, a piercing there and a few hippie halter tops. Decorations included posters of skeletons and roses and a bumper sticker that read MY REALITY CHECK BOUNCED. A jam band played on the corner stage. Live music is offered most nights; rarely is there a cover. When the stereo is on, expect Jerry and the boys, Dylan, et al. Music will be extinguished for reruns of The Family Guy.

Dive Rating: 3

Weed's

Hours: 4 p.m.–2 a.m., Monday-Friday; 7 p.m.–3 a.m., Saturday
Red Line to North and Clybourn

NORTH

Weed's is several strange bars rolled into one. For starters, visitors will be hard pressed to miss the bras and panties hanging on a wire around the bar. The practice started on Underwear Night, an evening when customers used to come with their intimates worn outside their clothes. On one such night, a patron hung up a brassiere, and the skivvies started to fly.

If you look harder, you'll find old shoes stuffed in odd places. These celebrate the bird portraitist John Audubon. Years back on Audubon's birthday, owner Sergio Mayora intended to bring stuffed birds to work. They proved too expensive. So he substituted a box of shoes found in the alley. Thus, "Birdbrains and Stupid Shoes Day" was born, as customers brought in old shoes, often stuffing them with poems. Since the city stopped allowing him to post flyers around the neighborhood, however, Mayora said both Underwear Night and Birdbrains and Stupid Shoes Day have ended.

Mayora is not hard to spot. He is the longhaired giant in dungarees and sunglasses who looks like the bust by the front window. When he greets friends he bows and kisses them on the hands. When asked for some exotic brand of tequila, he lies. "We've just run out of that," he says. "How about Cuervo?" It's the only tequila he sells.

Duct tape is Mayora's adhesive of choice. It's everywhere. It attaches a bra to the mounted hammerhead shark and keeps in place the Mexican blankets that cover the bar. By the bathroom, duct tape keeps scores of band flyers and marijuana decriminalization handbills from dropping to the floor. Odd decorations include a photograph of Pancho Villa that somewhat clashes with the many God Bless America stickers. A calm and peaceful Buddha meditates by the stage, and a poster of the oft-romanticized Che Guevara hangs on the same wall as a determined-looking Theodore Roosevelt.

My visit to Weed's was not pleasant. A blues band played blandly. A Johnny Cash cover nearly killed me, and I felt burned when forced to pay for it. I write "forced" because when the immense Mayora, touting a plastic pumpkin, tapped me on the shoulder and grunted for a band

CHICAGO'S BEST DIVE BARS

donation, I lost the courage to refuse. To top it all off, a shot of Jim Beam chased with a can of Old Style cost me seven extravagant dollars. The jam band jukebox is awful. Weed's usually hosts jazz on Thursdays, blues or rock 'n' roll on Fridays, open mikes on Saturdays and poetry slams on Mondays. On warmer days the deck is open.

Dive Rating: 3

Sporting Scene
Domino (pool, table tennis)
Fireside Bowl (bowling, football throwing)
Lincoln Square Lanes (bowling, darts, pinball, pool)
Shoes (darts, pool)
Marie's Riptide Lounge (electronic skeet shooting)

NORTHWEST

ALBANY PARK

AVONDALE

CRAGIN, HUMBOLDT PARK

JEFFERSON PARK

LOGAN SQUARE

MAYFAIR

OLD IRVING PARK,

Fireside Bowl

2646 W. Fullerton Avenue (Logan Square)
773-486-2700
Hours: Sunday-Saturday, 8 p.m.–2 a.m.
 # 74 Fullerton Avenue bus. The nearest El stop is the Blue Line California
stop closest to O'Hare.

New York Times columnist Dave Anderson once wrote that the Super Bowl should not be played outside in cold weather. "You want both teams at least to be able to perform at their best." Following a similar logic, I'll wager the World Bowling Championship will never be held at the Fireside. The slanted, un-oiled lanes send the chipped balls in unpredictable directions. The pinspotters frequently drop pins, and the sweepers don't always clean up the dead wood. When I last bowled there, only three of the sixteen lanes were working. I nabbed one right at the end, lane 16, where on the wall's sunset backdrop, a giant cartoon man speeds towards his pins, hand stuck to his ball. In the next lane sat a large garbage can. Farther down, young men and women danced around the scorer's table and threw balls at each other for laughs. But a lane costs only $10 an hour, so who fucking cares?

A crumbling playground for youth who dress in thrift-store castaways, with tattoos peeking through worn fabric, the Fireside is, in a word, seedy. Stalactite strings of dust dangle from the ceiling. The barstools are all ripped. The bar lists drinks and frozen pizza on handwritten boards, but the prices are not necessarily correct. Whatever you are charged, it won't be much. (On Monday's domestics cost $2.) Hammer, everybody's favorite bartender, is generally hilarious, though not always on purpose, as he frequently boasts in his trademark wheezy voice, "I'm going to the boats." Translation? Tonight he's gambling at a riverboat casino.

Past Hammer and the bar are the bowling lanes and a stage, which hosts mostly indie rock shows. (See www.mpshows.com for listings.) Black plywood walls, anchored by old automobile rims, keep the sweaty and grungy audiences off the lanes during performances.

I assume the Fireside Bowl was once a respectable bowling alley, packed with leagues of working-class men. These days it is like the episode of *Star Trek* when Captain Kirk and his cronies visit a planet where disease kills all the children when they hit puberty, leaving the young to run amok in the ruins of a city built by adults.

Dive Rating: 7 ⬤⬤⬤⬤⬤⬤

Fireside Bowl

Hangovers

Hangovers
3532 N. Pulaski Road (Old Irving Park)

Hours: 11 a.m.–2 a.m., Sunday-Friday; 11 a.m.–3 a.m., Saturday
Blue Line to Addison or ride the #53 Pulaski bus

A few bars are so ugly they deserve special note. Hangovers, where the décor hails from the Miami Vice school of design, is such a place. You'll fight the urge to snort cocaine right off the bar.

The counters in this northwest side eyesore are laminated in marbled plastic with tones of black and gray. Sparkly geometric shapes spot the walls. Plastered ceiling beams hang like boxy ribs and are outlined in black, like bad Keith Haring sculpture. Plaster-covered PVC pipes make awkward, unattractive light fixtures. Neon signs light beer posters of women in bikinis. A projection television flashes images on an immense, slightly swaying screen. The tavern's pièce de résistance shines behind the bar, where a corner chunk of counter space has been chopped off. In its place blooms an array of lights, glass shelves and bottles of booze that, for a week or two after installation, must have seemed the vanguard of style.

The jukebox has a smattering of rock and rap, even some Latino groups. Feeling the Miami heat I cooled off with a little "Against All Odds." I was promptly rewarded, as from across the room a man yelled thanks for playing the Phil Collins track and bringing the artist's collection to his attention.

As he went in for more Phil, I rambled over to the pool table. There thick-necked men communicated in grunts and clicks. Not understanding their tongue, I played just one game, wisely choosing to lose. They returned my courtesy by not beating me up.

In a bright, lonely room opposite the pool table and monitored by a hubcap-like security mirror, Hangovers sells booze and beer to go. Bottles are stacked up, floor to ceiling, along just one wall, with no aisles to hide behind when shoplifting (if that's your thing). If paying is your thing, prices are reasonable and written in marker. Hangovers also has video golf and video bowling.

I can't claim exotic adventure at Hangovers, though I did see a middle-aged woman in a pink track outfit with "Baby Doll" printed on her ass. I see promise, however, and respect the fact that at Hangovers, I'll never run into anyone I know.

Dive Rating: 9 ●●●●●●●●●

Domino

3905 W. Belmont Ave. (Avondale)

Hours: 7 a.m.–midnight, Friday-Saturday; 11 a.m.–midnight, Sunday
Blue Line to Belmont and walk west

Squeezed between a taqueria and a gift shop that sells a 4-foot-tall Garfield doll lies the shabby Domino. I offer you these landmarks because the place is not easy to find. The sign above the door advertises Old Style but not the bar's name. Of the two barred windows, one is smashed and won't be fixed soon. I wouldn't even have stopped in if the two men I'd cut off while driving hadn't gotten out of their car when I pulled over, then followed me down the sidewalk.

Once safely inside, I was slapped by the paint job: black, turquoise and pink. Ratty strips of carpets cover high-traffic areas, and shelves and cabinets are covered in ska band checkerboard. Nailed to the ceiling are pink and turquoise boards with cup-sized holes cut out, all of which give the place the look of the Joker's rec room from a '60s *Batman* episode.

But what a rec room. Domino boasts all the amenities—big-screen television (tuned to Polish satellite programming), pool table, dartboard and the prime find, table tennis. Hard bats are stored behind bar, and when I asked to see the paddles, a barfly challenged me to a game. I beat him soundly, though should have given him a handicap. In broken English he said he had drunk a gallon of vodka earlier that day.

Old Style cost $1 a draft, and the bartender, a blonde Pole, pours with a mixing bowl to catch overflow—must be something wrong with the equipment. She classed the place up with high heels and an all-black outfit and served with midriff exposed, the style for eastern European women who bartend (see also Hangovers, Loop Tavern, Zakopane).

Domino has the holiday lights required of every dive, except as a twist management keeps the lights turned off. Or perhaps they don't work. The men's room light switch also flipped to no effect, and when I tried the women's room (to avoid making a mess in the dark), a stubborn door refused my entry, perhaps rusted shut from disuse. Other delights include security cameras and a stamped metal objet d'art of a motorcycle, over the word "Domino." Experience such cultural richness for yourself.

Dive Rating: 9 ● ● ● ● ● ● ● ● ●

Helen's Two Way Lounge

2412 N. Milwaukee Avenue
(Logan Square)
773-227-5676

Hours: 7 a.m.–2 a.m., Monday-Friday; 7 a.m.–3 a.m.,
Saturday; 11:30 a.m.–2 a.m., Sunday
Blue Line to California (the one nearer O'Hare) or ride the #74 Fullerton bus

The first time I went to Helen's, a tiff between a swaying brunette and her friend seemed destined for trouble. The brunette was accused of drinking too much. She defended herself with raised voice as the whole bar listened. But at the critical moment she relented, ending the dispute not with fists, but with tears, a hug and the words "I just drink to have fun."

Two nights later I watched a white man with two Confederate flags— one on a tattoo, one on a bandana—yip and yelp and dance as he beat a black man in pool. The black man didn't look pleased. He made a phone call, and when two more black men entered the bar and stepped directly to the table, I all but dove for cover. But again, no fisticuffs. The men weren't here to fight. They just wanted the next game.

Customers come to Helen's because they live nearby. Taps of Bud for $1.25 are another good reason, and besides pool you can shoot darts and play table Pac-Man. The jukebox is jammed with country music, and inevitably a red-eyed couple ends up swinging. Though the dancing may not be pretty, something is so right about a tipsy pair turning to a sad slide guitar.

The toilets are also sad country. A picture of a cowboy marks the men's room door, a cowgirl the women's. One trip inside reminded me why I don't vacation at campgrounds.

Other atrocities are artistic. A sculpture of the Chicago skyline, a garish semblance of sheet metal and closet-organizer leftovers look as if designed by a man trying to quell his urge to kill. The skyline actually makes the catchpenny prairie house, hanging on another wall, seem marginally attractive. Yet tackier than both was the shirt the bartender tried to sell me. It cost $15 and read DRINK TILL YOU WANT ME.

Dive Rating: 7 ●●●●●●

Jefferson Inn

4874 N. Milwaukee Avenue (Jefferson Park)
773-283-5522

Hours: 3 p.m.–2 a.m., Sunday; 1 p.m.–2 a.m., Monday-Thursday;
2 p.m.–2 a.m., Friday; 2 p.m.–3 a.m., Saturday
Blue Line to Jefferson Park. A bus terminal across the street serves many
of the CTA bus lines.

There's not a whole lot happening in Jefferson Park. "My brother lives there," a friend told me. "It's in the city, but it's like a suburb. A bad suburb."

Before scouting the Jefferson Inn, I stopped at a bar just up the street. For an hour I was the only customer. It was a Saturday night. So I left and went on to my destination, where I joined a handful of weary men at the bar as we took turns admiring the bartender, the only girl in the Inn. I drank heavily, starting with beer, switching to Jack and ginger, then Jameson, then back to beer. When not watching the bartender, we watched an old Arnold movie on television and munched free peanuts and pretzels. One guy ordered a pizza and kindly shared. The manager spotted me a brew. A beer cost $2, a cocktail $3. As time went on and my buzz went up, more people arrived, even a few women, and near the windows a stocky fellow with studs in his face performed magic.

The bar has been family-owned for thirty years but boasts no interesting heirlooms, save some old movie posters, which look like replicas, and a tacky rendering of Al Capone lit by two fake flames. In back are a dartboard and a few booths. You've got to feed money into the jukebox if you don't want to hear the television, and a young man and I pooled our quarters for a few extra songs. He told me he was in love with a girl, but things between them weren't so hot. I picked a song just for him, and when "Wild Horses" came on he got teary-eyed, nodded in approval and headed to the men's room. He returned some minutes later and confessed that he had called his girlfriend. "You're not going to believe this," he said, "but I admitted to her that I've been stealing her underwear."

Dive Rating: 6 ●●●●●●

The Mutiny

2428 N. Western Avenue (**Logan Square**)
773-486-7774

Hours: 11 a.m.–2 a.m., Sunday-Friday; 11 a.m.–3 a.m., Saturday
#49 Western or #74 Fullerton bus

The chunk of porcelain that dominates the men's room at the Mutiny is what Ed, the owner, boasts is the world's largest functioning urinal. It's Herman Munster big, and gentlemen shouldn't fret if they feel small in its shadow. The bathroom walls are colored a ghoulish, sickly fuzzy green, and I asked Ed why he keeps his bathroom so nasty. "It stops people from writing graffiti." (Yeah, Ed, people wouldn't want to ruin your moldy walls.)

The Mutiny has two crowds—the older, after-work locals and the late-night, greasy-haired punks. Occasionally the two groups mix and bond over free pool, free video golf and dirt-cheap pitchers. Of the seven dartboards, I've never seen any played, though league nights are Tuesdays.

In back, amidst the clutter of dusty bottles, old tills, battered boxes and burned-out electronic equipment, stands a crude stage, lit by living-room track lighting. To set the right mood, a musician may reach up and unscrew a light bulb or shield it with a red plastic filter. Another special feature is the bar's hanging ceiling, many of whose tiles have been painted on by customers. One shows a beer bottle that reads, "Muff Beer: Born of Natural Woman—Official beer of the Fight Boyz." The fanged "Angry Pussy" is also an eye-catcher. Ask Ed if you're interested in designing your own.

The Mutiny's nautical references include a painting of a sea captain, a stuffed toy parrot, two model ships and a photo of a former mayor of Key West who led an attempt to secede the island from the United States. A Chicago native, Ed has always wanted to live in Florida or California. He said that's where his high-school buddies went, and he has always felt left behind. But now that artists hang out at his bar, his dreams may have changed. Throw in a parking lot and a 4 a.m. license, and Ed said he might stay forever.

Dive Rating: 8 ● ● ● ● ● ● ●

Lost & Found Lounge

3058 W. Irving Park Road
(Albany Park)
773-463-7599
Hours: I have no idea.
Brown Line or Blue Line to Irving Park then transfer to
the #80 Irving Park Rd. bus

3I drove with fingers crossed to the Lost & Found, hoping to unearth my first lesbian dive. I found it. And was kicked out fifteen minutes later.

From the outside, the Lost & Found doesn't look like a gay bar, or any bar. I drove by twice before spotting the low-key black and white sign. After I knocked a few times on the front door, I saw someone look through the tinted window, but no one let me in. I walked to the side of the building, looking for another entrance, then returned to the front. A woman trying for a clearer signal on her mobile phone exited, and I grabbed the door to get inside.

She stopped me and asked if I knew where I was. Yeah, I knew. She said it was women's dart league night. "All women's." "That's great," I said. "You don't understand," she countered. "This is a lesbian bar."

I brushed past her to find a bar so clean the floor shined, as if Sears Roebuck had started selling dives preassembled. The dominant color was brown, the dominant vintage 1970s. I spied a few tables, a jukebox and a solitary electronic dartboard—rather lean for a bar with such a serious league. I counted four men (so seeming) and ten women. Everyone wore pants.

Before I could remove my coat, a woman said in my face: "This is a private club. You're going to have to leave." I asked her what I had to do to stay, and she said I'd have to join the dart league. I asked how I might join and was directed to one of the men (so seeming). He shook my hand, smiled politely and ignored me. Seeing as I was having little luck with the league's commissioner, I asked what nights were non-league. "Saturday," she said. "Maybe." As this went on, I could hear another woman say, "He's got to leave. He's got to get out of here." Then the woman who had inadvertently let me in came to my rescue. "All this guy wants is a beer. Let him stay for a beer," she said.

The bar conceded me a beer, and when I ordered, the bartender smiled and complimented my cheekbones. I sat on a stool, and various people questioned me on my story. Why are you here? Where are you from? How did you find out about this place? Are you gay? I was told to relax. "There's nothing to be scared of," someone said.

Three people apologized for the way I was being treated. One woman said lesbians in this area—far from gay hubs such as Boystown and Andersonville—are particularly wary of strangers. Straight men sometimes stop in just to ogle lesbians. "And with the news these days . . . " she whispered, referring to four recent murders of gay men.

If I were gay or had visited the Lost & Found with a gay friend, I wager I would have wanted to stay. But as it happened, the oldest lesbian bar in the city treated me quite badly, making it hard for me to recommend.

Dive Rating: 4 ● ● ● ●

Live Music
Artis's (blues)
Baby Doll Polka Club (polka)
Cal's (punk)
Hideout (folk)
Fireside Bowl (indie rock)
New Apartment Lounge (jazz)
Velvet Lounge (jazz)

Moon's Bar & Liquor

2405 W. Chicago Avenue (Humboldt Park)
Hours: 7 a.m.–2 a.m., Monday-Friday; 7 a.m.–3 a.m.,
Saturday; 11 a.m.–3 a.m., Sunday
#66 Chicago Ave. or #49 Western Ave. buses

There's not much to say about Moon's except that I had the time of my life there.

This nondescript half bar, half liquor store is exactly what I was looking for when I agreed to write this book. Within fifteen minute of our entering, a shrill voice yelled, "Hey white boys," to me and a friend. "Put some white music in the jukebox before these Mexicans get to it." The yeller was a vulgar woman in a very large turquoise shirt who possessed the anatomical traits of a bean bag. She provided running commentary throughout the evening, insulting everyone—no matter how tough the customer—as her portly husband sat beside her, silent and smiling.

When I shot pool, the woman bellowed, "Where's the beef?" and "I haven't seen something so skinny since I ate Chinese noodles with chopsticks." I overheard her finish one monologue with "My uterus is still working." Moon's mostly Mexican crowd laughed along, and while my friend surprised them with his street Spanish, I gained their admiration by dominating the pool table, not easy to do given the standard Mexican rule: last pocket eight ball. As I kept winning—seven straight—the local tough guys started buying rounds, insisting I play them next. Not even a gringo *Soul Train* could draw derision, and when I left a Chicano in a sharp-edged Sox cap made me promise to return the next weekend for another game.

I asked about Hector, Moon's owner, and was told that he was not available for comment because he had recently been shot. Four times. Twice in the back, twice in the head. Somehow he was recovering. The events surrounding the shooting are hazy, but as the bartender said, "Obviously someone wants him dead."

I can't see why. He runs a fun bar, the kind of place where when you've bought a round, the bartender puts an upside down shot glass by your drink, credit for the next. Domestic beer costs $2, and when a woman leaves she hugs you and pecks you on the cheek. It's the kind of place you want to keep secret. And now I've let the secret out.

Dive Rating: 7 ●●●●●●○

Moon's Bar & Liquor

Podlasie Club

Podlasie Club

2918 N. Central Park Avenue (Logan Square)
773-276-0841

Hours: 7 a.m.–1 a.m., Monday-Friday; 7 a.m.–3 a.m.,
Saturday; noon–1 a.m., Sunday
Blue Line to Logan Square and transfer to the #53 Milwaukee Ave. bus.
Exit at Central Park Ave.

Most nights at Podlasie Club are dull—just a few guys drinking beer. But on Saturdays, local Poles storm the place like it's a senior (very senior) prom. Men wear suits. Women don sequined gowns. A lady with flour white skin checks coats at a booth, and a five-piece band wears starched whites as the well-dressed couples glide along the dance floor to slow Polish rock. A dive?

A dive! Pasted to a Michelob sign is a magazine advertisement for a sporty new convertible that is a good ten years out of production. Polish graffiti is scratched into the men's room door. Black lights conjure psychedelic rainbow patterns from the tables. Rocket tails of colored tinsel hang in bunches. The airbrushed murals—a pale moon rising over a chintzy Chicago skyline in one, lush vegetation swallowing an ancient colonnade in another—are a sight to behold. And, to top it all off, the bouffant hairdos worn by many of the female patrons screams tacky in both English and Polish.

I sat at the bar, across from a photo of a superimposed Pope John Paul II blessing Buckingham Fountain, the Chicago landmark. Everyone spoke Polish, and for the most part ignored me, but the bartender kindly kept tabs on my drinks. Aside from the gloriously cheesy band, the bulk of the entertainment came from a drunk who brought his bicycle inside the bar and parked it beneath the Britney Spears posters. The hostess became upset at this apparent breach of protocol, and with help from a friend who held open the door, she knocked the bike over and kicked it, five or six times, to the curb. The drunk protested loudly, and I took it as I sign that my trip to Podlasie was at an end.

Dive Rating: 6

Sidekicks

4424 W. Montrose Avenue (Mayfair)
773-545-6212
Hours: 2 p.m.–4 a.m., Monday-Friday; noon–5 a.m.,
Saturday; noon–4 a.m., Sunday
Blue Line to Montrose

Karaoke singers tend to be odd ducks, and Sidekicks has its fair share of misfits. The crowd comes in all shapes and sizes—none of them flattering—and likes to smoke. They're average joes, the anonymous kind you sit next to on the bus, but at night they are stars.

Some sing well, but most have mediocre voices, and a few could read the newspaper off-key. Good singers can get as bland as bad singers can get annoying. What I look for is showmanship and honesty. I've seen a young man of no great talent dedicate a song and hit notes that he had no business attempting, with the audience applauding wildly. I've heard giants with tiny voices and bores who pierce the poetry of song better than the pros. And a note to those who make the mistake of being obnoxiously ironic: Your friends may think you're funny, but everyone else thinks you're an asshole.

Don't go there early. Sidekicks doesn't fill until 10 p.m; by midnight the bar is bumping. The song line gets long, so pick out a tune as soon as you arrive. Binders with song lists are found on the tables, and the selection is phenomenal. Don't get overwhelmed. Pick a song, fill out a form (available at the DJ booth), and give it to Sally, the emcee, right away. Enjoy a $3 bottle High Life or a rail drink while you wait your turn.

If you're too chicken to sing, hum along and follow the lyrics on the five video monitors that dot the bar. Behold the strange videos that accompany some songs. Marvel as B-actors in period costumes perform odd plots whose connection to the actual songs is tenuous. I deeply suspect some bizarre industry code keeps video production teams purposely ignorant of the songs they film. The odd little films that result, with their Top 40 soundtracks sung live by amateurs, surpass the video installations at most major art museums.

The video for "You've Lost That Loving Feeling" is my favorite. As a middle-aged man butchers the song in real time, we see on the monitor a seaman at the fair with his girl. She isn't happy, and she's not trying hard not to show it. She fishes a cigarette out of her handbag, and the sailor fumbles with his Zippo as she impatiently waits. A sly carnival barker seizes the chance, and with a poof the end of his cane combusts into a five-inch flame. With lit cigarette and hair impossibly unsinged, the woman walks off with the carnie through smoke-machine mist. Just like I've always imagined.

Karaoke is an art, but the Sidekicks crowd seems bent on imitating the original. It is unfortunate. An open stage, background music and a microphone offer countless possibilities. I want more performances like that of Fat Tony, who during one performance took a fictitious mid-song telephone call on his mom's hefty old cell phone. Acts like this can rub audiences the wrong way, and the straight-laced emcee is likely to comment. (After energetic performances, she booms: "Somebody get that boy some decaf.") Remain humble, remember the little people, and you'll do fine.

Dive Rating: 5 ⬤⬤⬤⬤⬤

Stadium West/Sue's Wok On Inn Bar Kitchen

3188 N. Elston Avenue (Avondale)
773-866-2450
Hours: 11 a.m.–2 a.m., Tuesday-Sunday
Blue Line to Belmont

I always thought the pedestrian signals in Chinatown should read Wok, Don't Wok. Stadium West/Sue's Wok On Inn Bar Kitchen beat me to this horribly bad joke.

I found Stadium West—which is near no stadium, has two smallish TVs and whose claim to be a a sports bar is tenuous—by driving around aimlessly and stopping at the ugliest thing I could find. Inside nothing matched—not the people, not the food, not the jukebox, nothing. The color scheme includes gray, red, brown, beige, white, black and pink, along with a generous amount of flowers. The aroma of the abundant greenery tempers the smell of greasy Chinese dishes such as Cantonese fried shrimp and Hunan Beef. Non-Chinese fare includes Italian sausage, Pizza puffs and hot dogs. The kitchen closes at 9 p.m.

I played pool with a tough-looking man while his wife and young child waited at the bar. Games on the small crowded table cost 50 cents, and the balls move in arcs rather than straight lines. Past the video slot machine is an empty waste of space, and the only place to sit is on a barstool. The jukebox plays six songs for a buck.

Sue, the Chinese owner, both cooked and bartended but seemed happiest when playing video slots. She took little interest in serving drinks. Behind the bar, among an assortment of bad snapshots, stuffed singing bears and other trifles was a photocopied sheet detailing SEVEN REASONS WHY CHICAGO IS QUIET ON SUNDAY. Reasons include: the Mexicans are in the custody of the Immigration Department, the Blacks are in jail and the Puerto Ricans can't get their cars started. Jabs are also aimed at the Irish, Italians, Poles and Jews, and when I was caught copying the list by the bartender, Sue asked, "Do you like that? Everybody likes that." I lied and said yes. I was less offended and more amazed that the owner had tacked it up. I might have minded more if the list had bothered the Mexican eating egg drop soup. A Nicaraguan certainly found it funny. And another sign—I Can Only Please One Person Per Day and Today Isn't Your Fucking Day—put the list in better perspective. Management at

Stadium West doesn't hate some people. Management at Stadium West hates all people.

Dive Rating: 8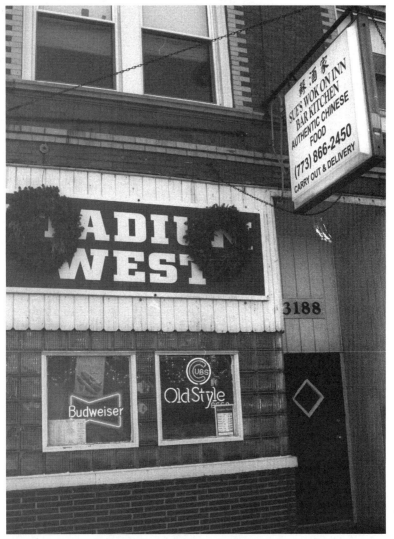

Stadium West/Sue's Wok On Inn Bar Kitchen

Pizza Lounge

2801 W. Chicago Avenue (Humboldt Park)
773-862-2834
Hours: 11 a.m.–10 p.m., Monday-Saturday
#66 Chicago Ave. bus

One night Chris, the owner and bartender at Pizza Lounge, proudly showed me a picture of himself, his wife and actor Keanu Reeves that stands on a shelf behind the bar. He pointed to Reeves and said, "That guy got me a new Chrysler."

Here's the story. Chris also owns Fast Food House, a restaurant next door to Pizza Lounge. One night a woman from Paramount came in and said she would pay him $10,000 to shoot a scene there for Hardball, a film about a Little League team from Cabrini Green. She rented his restaurant for two months, but the scene took only a few days. Cast, crew and equipment packed both the restaurant and Pizza Lounge. Wires ran along the bar. Huge fans cooled the restaurant. Police blocked off the streets. Business was great, but Chris (who calls police "coppers") saw an opportunity. He complained he had never agreed to rent out the bar—just the restaurant. The woman from Paramount offered him another grand. Chris consulted his wife. She said go for two. Her advice paid off. "I went out and bought that Chrysler the next day," he said.

Chris then showed me a second, older black-and-white photograph of a man standing sternly behind a bar, looking dapper in his apron, bowtie and bushy mustache. I imagined him polishing glasses with a towel. It was Chris's father at Pizza Lounge in 1939, and above him was a mural of a train. Back then the bar was called Hiawatha, after the famous Hiawatha passenger trains that raced on the tracks two blocks south. Chris said the train mural is still above the bar, but it is blocked by the lowered ceiling.

And for the answer to the obvious question, Pizza Lounge used to serve pizza, but the oven has long been turned off. These days the best deal is a can of Red Dog and a shot for $3. The special runs Monday to Thursday, perhaps for good reason. Fridays is payday, when the predominately working-class clientele comes in to cash paychecks, celebrate and dream, perhaps, of owning their own brand-new Chrysler.

Dive Rating: 7 ●●●●●●●

Tap Room/Foremost Liquors

3210-12 N. Cicero Avenue (Cragin)
773-282-6064

Hours: 11 a.m.–10 p.m., Sunday; 7 a.m.–10 p.m.,
Monday-Thursday; 7 a.m.–11 p.m., Friday & Saturday
Blue Line to Belmont and transfer to the westbound #77 Belmont bus

There are plenty of reasons not to come to the Tap Room. A few off the top of my head:

No one cool will ever come here
No cool band will ever play here.
No odd gimmick makes this a place you've got to see.
A celebrity will not be stopping by.
It isn't pretty.
It isn't quaint.
It isn't fun.

Well, maybe the last one isn't true. I've stopped here exactly once, on a bone-cold Friday in January. I was looking for a polka lounge and found a used-car lot where the lounge was used to be. After a few other dead ends, I ended up at the Tap Room.

As I sat down, a man hollered, "This sucks!"

"Life sucks," a woman with a face like a road map replied. "Get used to it."

We were served by a Polish gal—a real giant, the kind you fight the urge to buy a cigar for. A couple of video games—bowling and golf—added something, though I am not sure what, and to promote an international feel or perhaps to settle disputes, someone had pinned up a map of the world. There were lots of beer signs, a sign telling you not to flush paper towels down the toilet, a "parking for Polish only" sign and a sign that read, "I don't drink in your bed, so please don't sleep in my bar." Lots of signs at the Tap Room, few signs of life.

As I left I noticed a quiet, odd awkward man wearing earphones. His open backpack sat on the table, and in it I could see an aged newspaper with Princess Di smiling on the cover. Behind it was a stack of similar old papers, all carefully bound. I don't know what it all means, but somehow it sums up the Tap Room.

Dive Rating: 8 ⬤⬤⬤⬤⬤⬤⬤⬤

Whirlaway Lounge 3224 W Fullerton Avenue (Logan Square)
773-276-6809

*Hours: 3 p.m.–2 a.m., Sunday-Friday; 3 p.m.–3 a.m., Saturday (open
Sunday at noon during football season)
The Blue Line Logan Square stop is a short walk away, but the #74
Fullerton Ave. bus will drop you at Whirlaway's door.*

If you introduce yourself to Maria the first time you drink at Whirlaway Lounge, on your second visit she'll greet you by name. Maria, who bartends and owns the lounge with her husband Sergio, might better use her massive memory to count cards. But instead she wastes her talent making us lost souls feel at home. We're thankful for that.

Maria has kept things calm at the Whirlaway for twenty-three years. She lives with her family in a house behind the bar, and a door from the bar leads to the apartment above. I've seen Maria's son exit through that door with two friends, each stopping to lean over the bar and kiss Maria's cheek. On the walls hang photo collages of customers and friends enjoying birthdays at the bar. They are the kind worth looking at only to see if you're in them.

Besides being clean and too goddamn friendly, Whirlaway isn't remarkable. The jukebox is decent and the drinks are cheap. There's a couch, a pool table and two televisions. The clientele is mostly hip and young, with a smattering of old regulars who have lived in the neighborhood for years. On Tuesday nights the lounge has a free buffet. The night I went the place was packed, and I had to eat standing up. I'm not sure what I ate—some potatoes, ground meat and a vegetable or two—but there was plenty to choose from, and it tasted better than anything in my refrigerator at home. There's also an annoying amount of popcorn at Whirlaway, bothersome in that just when you think you've finished with the stuff, Maria fills your tub yet again. Maria also likes her ashtrays clean, so don't be surprised if you go through seven or eight fresh ashtrays before you finish your smoke.

The bar is best on a Saturday night. There's a good crowd but still room to sit and drink. That's when I met the drill sergeant who told me how he used a bottle of butane and a lit cigarette to persuade a stubborn recruit to stay in the army. We drank near the entrance, and Sarge said he always sat here so he could escape in case "something went down." I asked him what he meant. He said, "If I would have been in the E2 [night club disaster], I would have ` out. I would have stabbed my way to the door." He was joking. Sort of.

Rating: 4 ●●●●

SOUTH

BACK OF THE YARDS

CALUMET HEIGHTS

CHATHAM

GRAND CROSSING

GRESHAM

HYDE PARK

SOUTH CHICAGO

WOODLAWN

Artis's

1249 E. 87th Street (Calumet Heights)
773-846-5467

Hours: 11 a.m.–2 a.m., Sunday-Friday; 11 a.m.–3 a.m., Saturday
#87 bus to the Red Line

There is an old Chinese proverb "The dirtier the kitchen, the better the food." A similar logic exists at Artis's: "The uglier the bar, the better the booze."

A blues bar in Calumet Heights, Artis's possesses an interior that is a disaster. Some of its walls are covered in buckling wood paneling; others are plaster and sport strange geometric forms that in the bluish light seem gray and green and red all at once. Over the V-shaped bar hang bizarre demi-walls, painted in some impossible soupy color. Between them are brass glass racks, wrapped in blue and pink neon, which glare off the creamy Formica counters. On the front wall, two steers, engraved on mirrors, face each other, their legs severed so as not to block the windows. The only decorations of aesthetic note are the framed photographs of soul bands, who dress in identical, all-white tuxedos.

Since nothing matches, though, nothing is out of place. Not the tops of cocktails covered with napkins, cocktail straws poking through like periscopes. Not the beer bottles bundled in paper jackets that soon turn soggy. The customers, a jubilant bunch, often keep their own gaudy glasses. Some are painted. Others are studded with glass gems that spell out a name or nickname. (I sat next to a Rodney.) In the rickety men's room, there's no soap dispenser. One dips a finger into a lowball glass of pink liquid as if it were a font of holy water.

On Mondays, blues buffs stop in to hear Billy Branch & the Sons of Blues. The crowd becomes a bit more mixed (I've met tourists from Tokyo here, but this place isn't touristy) and teems with musicians. The music is as authentic as the blues gets, and the band begins at about ten o'clock, while Mr. Branch, a hot harpist, readies himself with a few drinks at the bar. To pay for the band, drink prices jump far past acceptable dive levels, so if you are cheap come on Friday, when a DJ spins soul and R&B. The patrons can be quite lively, pounding the bar, dancing, cheering and singing. You may be asked to join in, but if you don't know the dance (called stepping on the South Side), decline. As one lady said to me, "Don't let those girls make a fool out of you."

Dive Rating: 6 ●●●●●○

The Cove

1750 E. 55th Street (Hyde Park)
773-684-1013
*Hours: 10 a.m.–2 a.m., Monday-Thursday; 11 a.m.–2 a.m., Friday;
11 a.m.–3 a.m., Saturday; noon–2 a.m., Sunday
The #6, #55 and #172 are just a few of the buses that will get
you near the Cove*

The Cove aims for a nautical theme, but its aim is not too good. Besides ship-wheel chandeliers, some whale-shaped coat hooks and an old harpoon above the bar, this may as well be any landlubber's drinking spot. But it's the best Hyde Park has to offer.

A tall, blazing sign makes the Cove hard to miss, and inside, behind the crescent-shaped bar, a segmented mirror reminds one of the final fight scene in Enter the Dragon. Customers drink beer and play chess in back. There's a dartboard and a pinball machine as well. On Tuesdays, pitchers are a dollar off, so the place is overrun with University of Chicago students.

On the jukebox there's Guns N' Roses and the Velvet Underground, and on my last visit the entire bar sang the Beatles' "Come Together," to my great distress. The ringleader of the sing-in announced, "I've got my mojo working! Aren't you glad I didn't leave?" Another collaborator cried, "This place is rocking now!" I nearly reached for my coat, but stayed and spoke with Speedy, a patron since 1967. The zippy jazz pianist told me how he used to play at the Cove before they took the piano away. As another Beatles song teed-up on the jukebox and the crooners cleared their throats, I thought it was a good time to bring the piano back. NOW!

Dive Rating: 5

Bob's Place Lounge

745 E. 75th Street (Chatham)
773-488-1355

Hours: noon–4 a.m., Sunday-Friday; noon–5 a.m., Saturday
Red Line to 79th then transfer to the #75 bus

Within a minute of my entering Bob's, a buxom woman, her warm breasts on my back, was rubbing my neck and asking if I wanted to step. I wasn't sure what she meant. Then I found out. And it wasn't what I thought. Stepping is popular among South Side blacks. Not to be confused with the vigorous step shows put on by black fraternities in the South, the stepping at Bob's is a smooth, slow dance where couples turn and cut and dip to R&B. There are even stepping bands. I turned down the woman's offer ("Anytime you feel like dancing, baby, you just find me"), but I watched her glide all evening, arms around yet another one of Bob's men.

But Bob's is not just a dance club. With tinsel, bouquets of hearts and a long red Formica bar, it has a tarnished chic that just screams dive. Patrons dress well, the men sporting at the very least clean shirts and slacks, others dressed to the nines, in dazzling suits, the women in revealing little numbers.

The crowd is a friendly bunch—even though they kept telling me I had nothing to worry about as far as my safety, which of course kept me on edge all night. It didn't help that I had an escort when I went to get a pack of cigarettes at the gas station around the corner. When I got back, a stranger bought me an Old Grand-Dad on the rocks and introduced me to all of his friends. He kept saying how he likes Bob's (and how safe it is) because it is so racially mixed. For once I felt as if I were adding a bit of cultural diversity to the world.

Dive Rating: 8

Bob's Place Lounge

Drop Inn Lounge

Drop Inn Lounge

551 E. 79th Street (Chatham)

Hours: 10 a.m.–2 a.m., Monday-Friday; 10 a.m.–3 a.m., Saturday;
11 a.m.–2 a.m., Sunday
Red Line to 79th and transfer to the #79 bus

I was out with a friend, and earlier we had stopped at a nearby spot that hosts Sunday night jazz. It had been crowded, noisy and bright. Conversation was impossible and we had to keep stepping aside as people shuffled by. My nerves frayed. I wanted privacy. At the Drop Inn we found it.

The jukebox was off, and only a quiet murmur came from the television. We sat down at the jagged bar, which is shaped like a squashed M, and were greeted by a yawn. The bartender was on the second half of a double shift. She served us, then returned to the evening news, leaving us to marvel at the red all around us. The Drop Inn Lounge is dominated by its paint job, a pattern of primitive red slashes that look like the marks of a madman ticking off days. Cracked and crooked light fixtures bathe the bar in a bloody glow, and the only thing missing from the ragged red carpet is a chalk outline. I noticed glitter on the walls when some turned up in my drink. Mirrors on two long walls make this slender lounge look wider than it is, and through a series of reflections I watched a couple talk over bottles of Heineken, served South Side style with napkins wrapped around the tops. It was Easter Sunday and the woman wore a fancy dress, the man a purple suit. A purple hat covered his jerry curl.

Over the course of the next hour, several more well-dressed customers stopped in, some saying hello to us. One man walked in and asked for the night's lotto numbers. The bartender recited them by heart. My friend and I had a long, quiet and uninterrupted chat. With no trends, no styles and little chatter, the Drop Inn Lounge is the perfect place to have a peaceful talk. Even if it looks like a murder scene.

Dive Rating: 9

Flamingo Cocktail Lounge

6644 S. Cottage Grove Avenue (Woodlawn)
773-684-0600
Hours: 11 a.m.–2 a.m. Sunday-Friday; 11 a.m.–3 a.m. Saturday
Green Line to East 63rd/Cottage Grove and walk south

I was on the South Side to visit Jimmy's Woodlawn Tap, a Hyde Park bar where I was told I would find scruffy old men with staggering intellects. What I found instead was a college bar, owned by the University of Chicago, that had little going for it. The conversations I struck up were dull, and a particularly boring exchange with two coeds painfully reminded me that no matter how lauded a university may be, a degree, in many respects, is just a piece of paper.

But the dullness of the college kids stirred in me a sense of adventure, and against the caution of white and black friends alike, I headed south from Hyde Park to find out what drinking is like on the other side of the tracks. Soon I was inside the Flamingo.

My friend and I received a few stares when we were buzzed inside— we're both white. My friend asked a gentleman by the door, "Are we cool?" A little surprised, the man replied in the affirmative, and before long he had his arms around us as we laughed and enjoyed drinks.

Cocktails are concocted by Carol, a quick-witted graceful lady who dresses in a black vest and bow tie. She's said to be in the bartender's hall of fame, so to test her I ordered an old-fashioned. It was miserable. In Carol's defense, she didn't have the proper ingredients and told me so. That does not, however, excuse the substitution of dry vermouth for bitters, a replacement bordering on criminal. When I asked for extra cherries in a vain attempt to better my horrible drink, Carol warned the ladies that I was a young man who had an appetite for cherries. She would razz me like that the rest of the night, to the delight of my friend.

As the night wore on, I felt more and more at ease. My friend danced with a prostitute, and Carol and I settled on the name of our new drink: the cherry bomb. A man said we had big balls to walk into Flamingo, but it didn't feel that way. Sure it's a tough part of town, but you garner a certain amount of respect just for coming in.

Dive Rating: 8 ●●●●●●●●

Lee's Unleaded Lounge

7401 South Chicago Avenue (Grand Crossing)
773-493-3477
Hours: 8 p.m.–2 a.m., Daily
Red Line to 69th to the #30 South Chicago bus

As you head to Lee's Unleaded Lounge, a South Side juke joint, you'll pass boarded-up houses, gloomy factories and the long corrugated fence of a junkyard. Two rail lines, the Illinois Central and Norfolk Southern, sandwich this blighted industrial corridor, and in abandoned lots, trees and brush tangle with garbage. A nearby bar is closed down, and just when you think its time to turn back toward civilization, the oddly shaped Lee's, on the sharp corner of 74th Street and the diagonal South Chicago Avenue, juts out its chin like a cocky boxer.

Lee's was once a dump itself. But in 2001 longtime customer Stanley Davis bought the bar and remodeled. The red carpet was ripped off the walls, and the stained ceiling tiles were torn down. Davis painted the walls black and installed professional stage lights and speakers. He moved the stage to create more intimacy and remodeled the bathrooms.

A former state police lieutenant, Davis aspires to make Lee's a landmark for the blues. He frequently boasts of articles in *Men's Journal* and *National Geographic* that mention Lee's, but don't think Davis is selling his bar out; he still operates Lee's in a style that befits blues and the South Side. From his stool by the register, he enthusiastically works the crowd. Between sets, he announces birthdays and welcomes out-of-towners. He gives a shout out to bluesmen in the audience—there's Junk Yard Dog, there's Arkansas Belly Roll—and musicians are welcome to sit in onstage. I felt sympathy for guitarist Phil Guy, who must by sick of being introduced as blues legend Buddy Guy's brother. And yet I also felt envy—not for his still sizable fame, but for Mr. Guy's gray leather suit. In between sets, a resident blues diva revs the crowd up by playing "The Cha Cha Slide" on the jukebox.

The neighborhood may be dicey, but the doorman will take care of you. I'd feel comfortable taking my mom here. In the mean time, watch yourself. You may be sitting next to a legend.

Dive Rating: 4 ●●●●

Goal Post II Cocktail Lounge

938 E. 75th Street (Grand Crossing)
773-651-6951

Hours: 3 p.m.–2 a.m. Sunday, Tuesday-Friday; 3 p.m.–3 a.m., Saturday
Red Line to 79th and transfer to the eastbound #75 bus

It was Mother's Day and the Goal Post II Cocktail Lounge was packed. The bartender handed out roses. I was alone and underdressed, nursing my hangover with beer and regretting that I hadn't called my mom. I rested my elbows on the turquoise padding that runs the length of the bar and looks like Naugahyde toothpaste squeezed from a giant tube. To my left a man placed a napkin over his fresh cocktail then asked me to watch his drink. He went to the men's room, where ones feet sink into the rotten floor. When he returned he thanked me and said one can never be too careful.

On my right a heavy woman approached like a tanker making port. She carried a large handbag, a plate full of soul food and a rose, and once positioned on her stool, she inched herself to the bar, nudged by unseen tugboats. I looked at her plate, which was packed with green beans, macaroni and cheese, ham and fried chicken. She pointed to tables by the dance floor. "The food is free," she said.

I had already eaten dinner, but I couldn't resist. The woman who loaded up my plate laughed and asked, "This the first time you had soul food?" The fried chicken was delicious, and my belly swelled over my belt. As I ate, a big man stopped at my barstool, put his hand on my shoulder and asked, "How's it going white boy?"

A photographer appeared with an old Polaroid camera and charged couples to take their pictures. A woman in white—very poised and proper—sold raffle tickets for a dollar. The prize was a Mother's Day gift basket. Two marketers promoted menthol cigarettes and gave away free packs. The DJ announced their arrival and departure, and when they left the bar gave them an ovation. The DJ played "The Cha Cha Slide," and everyone danced in unison.

Goal Post II is a sequel to the original Goal Post Cocktail Lounge on 71st Street. The woman with the plate of soul food hosts social events at Goal Post I, so I asked her about it. She whispered, "The drinks are better there."

Dive Rating: 7

Lemelle's

1801 W. 87th Street (Gresham)

Hours: noon–9 p.m., Sunday-Tuesday; noon–2 a.m., Wednesday-Friday;
noon–3 a.m., Saturday
Red Line to 87th and transfer to the #87 bus

SOUTH

When I pushed on the front door of Lemelle's, I was surprised to find it opened. From the outside, this dumpy dive looks closed for good. The old sign flakes paint and doesn't light up at night. Caged dirty windows shroud the dark interior.

Once inside I ducked. No, a ruffian wasn't waiting to slug me. It was the old men with failing eyesight, whipping darts sidearm at the electronic dartboard by the door, that spooked me. Lemelle's boasts a litany of other hazards, including mirrored ceiling tiles that look destined to crash on your head and mixed drinks that could knock out a moose. A $5 vodka cranberry was measured out like this: a thimble of ice, a shot of Absolut that peaked over the 2 oz. line, another such shot, a splash more vodka for good measure and a solitary drop of juice. People polished off these deadly drinks without so much as a grimace; then, at waist-high tables shaped like a dog's bone, they argued about who had the next round. I sat at the Smurf blue bar that resembled the deck of a pontoon boat. With my elbows I leaned on the bar's rail, and it sagged beneath the weight. I am not a big man.

Lemelle's caters to an older crowd; in fact, a sign says that the bar only serves those twenty-five years of age and older. Technically, I don't think this is legal, but that doesn't stop bars from maintaining the policy, which supposedly keeps out young thugs. I wish it had kept out one woman in particular, who subjected me to the worst story ever told. For twenty awful minutes, I listened to her explain how she liked to be called by her full first name—no short cuts, no nicknames, just her full first name. She attacked this red-hot issue from every conceivable and not conceivable angle, and when she finally finished I was ready for the grave. But unbelievably, she hadn't even gotten to the actual story yet, an excruciating tale of a cross-country trip and a stolen Porsche. I could hear the car's odometer flipping as she talked and talked. And talked.

As I suffered, the owner sat by quietly and watched television. Occasionally my pleading eyes drifted to him, but he would not save me. He just sat there in a "Support the Troops" sweatshirt that looked a few wars behind. So I listened and listened. And listened.

Dive Rating: 8

Linda's Place

1044 W. 51st Street (Back of the Yards)

Hours: 5 p.m.–2 a.m., Sunday-Friday; 11 p.m.–3 a.m., Saturday
Red Line to 47th and transfer to the eastbound #51 bus

In his essay "Who's Got the Blues?" David Hajdu asks whether or not blues music has been co-opted by whites. He describes how, having escaped the crowds at the Chicago Blues Festival, he relaxed at Linda's Place: "To the right of the bar, a quartet played a set of soft jazz and soul ballads, while one couple slow-danced. I was the only white person there—until around 11 o'clock."

"Then," he writes, "carloads of people, none of them African American, began emptying into Linda's, and the place changed. The band, apparently anticipating the onslaught, dropped the soul-jazz in favor of gut-bucket blues warhorses like 'Sweet Home Chicago' and brought on a vocalist, L-Roy Perryman, a brassy showman in a blue jumpsuit who bellowed and strutted through the crowd. . . . By midnight, Linda's was packed tight. I counted thirty-seven white faces."

Based on my experience at Linda's, Hajdu is dead wrong. Crowds at South Side juke joints are, for the most part, black, and if tourists roll in for the night, so be it. (Could the predominately white crowd on the night Hadju describes have been there because of the Blues Festival?) And Hadju's version of Perryman playing to a white crowd seems very similar to his performance the night I saw him at Linda's, when everyone but me was black.

Sociology aside, I like Linda's better when the music is off. I like talking to Bubblegum the bartender and her friend about parking tickets and crooked cops, as thunderstorms rumble through the city and the news reports on flash floods.

So come for the blues if you wish, whether you are black or white. The music's not bad. But I come for Bubblegum. And a sign in the men's room that says, "Aim for the urinal, not the floor."

Dive Rating: 7

Michelle's

6317 Martin Luther King Drive (Woodlawn)
Hours: 1 p.m.–10 p.m., Sunday-Thursday;
1 p.m.–11 p.m., Friday-Saturday
Green Line bound for East 63rd–Cottage Grove and exit at King Drive

Comedian Chris Rock says no matter what city you're in, you don't want to be on Martin Luther King Drive. I disagree.

Admittedly, 63rd and King is a tough part of town. Though Hyde Park mansions and high rises are just north, the streets here are littered with trash. The rumble of the El can sound menacing, like it's trying to muffle a scream. A friend who came along with me asked where she could go to buy cigarettes and was told by a stranger, "You don't want to be out this time of night. Here, just take some of mine." We also saw a car at a stop sign with no driver. It had been abandoned.

And yet once I entered Michelle's, a tiny little lounge without a sign, I felt more welcome than at bars I'd frequented for years. Strangers shook my hand and insisted on buying me and my friend a round. The bartender asked my name and remembered it later. I met a wonderful man named Earl and a woman who called everybody Sugar. Neither cared who we were or what we were doing there. All they wanted was a smile in return for the smile they gave us.

Michelle's fits all the dive bar criteria. Walls are made of everything—flimsy wood, dirty plaster and mirrors of all shapes. A high border repeats the pattern of a backgammon table, and icicle lights rain down from the ceiling. White cocktail tables are shaped like the heads of deformed tennis rackets. Bathrooms are flypaper brown. Bottles of Guinness are normally $3, though drink prices went up a quarter another night I was there, when Butch the DJ was spinning records.

If you've got the guts to come here, Michelle's may force you to question some of your deepest assumptions.

Dive Rating: 9

New Apartment Lounge

504 E. 75th Street (Chatham)
773-483-7728

Hours: noon–4 a.m., Sunday-Friday; noon–5 a.m., Saturday
Red Line to 79th Street, then transfer to the #75 bus

New Apartment Lounge is known outside its South Side neighborhood because of one man: Von Freeman. The Chicago tenor saxophonist plays here every Tuesday at 10:30 p.m., opening the evening with a long set. As he plays with his group, other musicians wait in the wings, some lined up against the wall with their instruments. When Freeman finishes, the open jam begins, and the assembled musicians then get a chance to try to impress the master.

Branford Marsalis said in *Grammy Magazine,* "It's one of those things you have to do while in Chicago—check out the Sears Tower, Michael Jordan's statue outside the United Center, go to the Lyric Opera [and] jam with Von Freeman." Marsalis also said the Freeman jam sessions are "the only place left in the world that represents what the scene was like in its heyday." What Marsalis doesn't mention is that New Apartment Lounge is a dump.

Once you see its unlit painted sign on 75th Street you'll realize the lounge is anything but new. Inside you'll find three very dated rooms from the funk era. Each has its own color—red, orange, blue—and each operates like an independent bar. The red room, closed most of the week, hosts reggae bands on weekends. The orange room, the most lounge-like of the three, handles overflow from other neighborhood bars and often doesn't get busy until 2 a.m. A sign in the orange room promotes the Wednesday "after work set" with DJ Dr. Feel Good, explaining, "There's no we without you."

I came for the jazz in the blue room. I had been told to arrive early, and at 9 p.m. I walked into a near empty bar. The bartender started my tab, and I watched the news with the only other customer, an old man in a suit. At 10:30 p.m. when the music started, the crowd was standing-room-only. Some sat on the floor. Others sat in the orange room and peered in through the entranceway.

The crowd included music nerds, couples dressed up, a guy in hospital scrubs, a few hipsters, students, locals, people young and old, black and white. Next to me two men talked about jazz. One of them asserted that the musical picture painted by Freedman onstage was not being filled in by the drummer and bassist accompanying him. They were drifting away, he said, getting lost in their own riffs. The man had come armed with drumsticks, and when he took over on the skins he forgot his own advice. His solo drifted out into space, and he was forced to stop and "one-two-three-four" to reel himself back in.

I waited with the drummer's friend and told him that I'd been searching all over Chicago for a scene like this. "Yes, it can be like this," he said, "and it can only be like this here."

Dive Rating: 9 ● ● ● ● ● ● ● ● ●

4 a.m.–ers
Bob's Place Lounge
Carol's Pub
Jackhammer
Lady Di's Pad
Lakeview Lounge
Marie's Riptide Lounge
New Apartment Lounge
Old Town Ale House
Touché

New Simpson's Lounge

2601 E. 83rd Street (South Chicago)
773-734-3301

Hours: 11 a.m.–2 a.m., Sunday; 10 a.m.–2 a.m. Monday-Friday;
10 a.m.–3 a.m., Saturday
This is a difficult place to reach at night. Take the Red Line to 79th and
transfer to the #79 bus. Exit at Colfax and walk south to 83rd Street.

Searching for bars in the southeast, I started at Roosevelt Road, not far from the Loop. I drove south on State Street through Bronzeville, then moved east before turning south at Martin Luther King Drive, passing high rises and old gray stone houses. I didn't pass a single bar.

I crossed under a railroad overpass in Hyde Park and crept southeast along the lakeshore, past the Midway Plaisance Park and Jackson Park to South Shore. I followed the Metra tracks that split Exchange Avenue and end in South Chicago. I didn't pass a single bar.

At 83rd Street I turned right, and after a half dozen blocks I saw through my road-salt encrusted windows a tall yellow sign for a single bar—New Simpson's Lounge.

I parked in front of a yard sign that said, "Gangs are not allowed. Drugs are not allowed. Drivers are asked to turn their music down. Cars cannot be washed in the street." Entering Simpson's through a side door with shattered glass, I was greeted by bewildered stares—a reaction that's hard to get used to—and a tin ceiling decorated with gold stars. I was wondering if I should get back in my car and retrace my route homeward when I met Sonny Boy, the self-proclaimed mayor of 83rd Street, a happy old man with salt-and-pepper hair and a limp.

"I was a good third baseman," he said. "Then I got shot [in Vietnam]. I still don't know what the fuck we were doing over there."

Sonny wanted to play pool, but the bar was out of quarters. He collected some from other customers, and combined with the few in my pocket, we had enough for two games. During the first match, a man with gold chains and rings approached me. "Did you bring your gun?" he asked. "They don't want guns in here." He was an off-duty cop, and he and the rest of the bar thought I was as well. As I explained myself, his hand expertly searched beneath my sport coat.

After that, the room warmed up to me. A girl helping out behind bar introduced herself and said she had been home-schooled, had finished her Bachelor's by the age of eighteen, held two Master's degrees and currently worked at the University of Chicago. I was impressed. A young man then opened the door and from the sidewalk announced his mother's birthday. Mom and friends stumbled in shortly after. Later on the birthday crowd sang along to 50 Cent: "Go, go, go shorty / It's your birthday . . . "

New Simpson's Lounge is ragged and worn, just how I like it. Half way up the walls are tassels of gold paper and silver foil. A large grill by the pool table cooks food for parties, and a collection of amps, cords and microphones waits by the front window. The lady who runs the joint is a doll. She asked me to come back—and to bring some of my people with me. I will, and I'll try.

Dive Rating: 9 ●●●●●●●●●

Norma's Lounge   2727 E. 92nd Street (Calumet Heights)

Hours: 11 a.m.–2 a.m., Sunday-Friday; 11 a.m.–3 a.m., Saturday
Norma's Lounge is near the Metra Electric Line's South Chicago station
and the CTA's #30 and #95E bus lines

During my evening at Norma's Lounge I was told by various people that I was Chicago PD, FBI, DEA, that I must be working on a class project, that I was lucky I hadn't been shot and that I had brass balls. When I finally told one man the truth, that I was writing a book, he said, "If you are writing a book, write the truth. Tell them what really happened in Vietnam." He then recited a litany of tragedies regarding that war.

Norma's Lounge is on 92nd Street, a block west of the Chicago Skyway, and is built like a bomb shelter—cinder block walls, few windows. The crowd is loud and a mix of ages. Above the men's room urinal hangs a poster of Janet Jackson in a bikini. A DJ plays music in the corner.

Upon my arrival I ordered scotch, and when I tried to switch brands for my second drink, the bartender warned me to stick with what I'd started with. As I sat at the banana-colored bar sipping a scotch I didn't want, a woman thrust a box of candy in my face.

"No, thank you," I said.

"It's for the children," she said through a mouth that lacked several front teeth. Throughout the rest of the evening, as she continually adjusted her bra, she tried without success to get me (and most of the bar) to buy her a drink. Giving up, she reached into her shirt and pulled out a wad of money wrapped in worn Manila paper—the children's fund. The children bought her a $2.25 bottle of Bud.

Later in the evening the owner bought me a drink. I wanted a beer, but he refused. He would only buy me scotch, and the bartender obliged with three long tilts of the bottle into my glass. At last call he bellowed, "Everybody's got to go. Tonight we closin' white-boy style." He paused and looked at me. "No offense."

Dive Rating: 10 ●●●●●●●●●●

SOUTHWEST

ARCHER HEIGHTS

GARFIELD RIDGE

WEST LAWN

Baby Doll Polka Club

6102 S. Central Avenue (Garfield Ridge)
773-582-9706
Hours: 4 p.m.–2 a.m., Monday-Friday; 7 p.m.–3 a.m., Saturday;
4 p.m.–2 a.m., Sunday
#63W bus to Central Avenue

On a cold night in January I entered the Baby Doll Polka Club to find Eddie Korosa Jr. onstage, squeezing out a Patsy Kline tune on his accordion, accompanying himself with a Casio synthesizer. He was between verses, and as I removed my coat and shook off the cold, he called out, "Hey! How ya doing?" That's Korosa, the kind of man who says heck instead of hell. He owns Baby Doll and plays most nights, either solo or with his band, His Boys from Illinois. He took over the club from his father, Eddie Sr., who passed away in 1998.

Midway Airport is just next door, so you'll also find heaps of aeronautical memorabilia—airline stickers, photos and models of jets. Airport employees stop in to tip cold ones after work, and passengers sometimes cab over for a quickie between connecting flights. High windows up front make the club a prime place to watch air traffic, though the view isn't as clear as it used to be. Across Central Avenue, the airport's western boundary, the city has built a long gray "blast wall" that dampens the roar of jet engines.

Wood beams the color of chocolate crisscross over the airy bar. Near the compact stage and dance floor are darling little cocktail tables, and the mirrors are marbled with vanilla frosting. The bathrooms shimmer with gold wallpaper and sparkling paint. The entire club is white-glove clean. Make a mess and you may get grounded.

While I was there, I had the pleasure of watching a pie-eyed old timer have his way with a fellow senior. As Korosa spurred them on, the man tossed about his giddy partner about the dance floor. When they spun apart he would lose her, and in a polka fog he would turn like a radar tower until he found her again. Amidst the mayhem, the woman beamed, though her smile could be seen only in glimpses. When the man brought her close, she was buried, and one could see only a puff of white hair cradled in his arms.

Dive Rating: 2

Trojanek's Lounge

4216 W. 63rd Street (West Lawn)
773-767-0909

Hours: 2 p.m.–2 a.m., Sunday-Friday; 2 p.m.–3 a.m. Saturday
Orange Line to Midway and transfer to the #63 bus

Nightlife in West Lawn is as insular as its cookie-cutter single-family homes. However, because 1) I needed another bar near Midway, and 2) it's chintzier than the competition, Trojanek's is included in this book.

Trojanek's is easily spotted on 63rd Street, as colored floodlights brighten the exterior—a series of sharp, angled walls—and a beer sign peeks through a single window. Inside a huge rectangular bar dominates the room. Half of the bar's walls are covered with sheets of fake bricks, the others smeared with coffee-colored plaster. Little sparkles shine from its thick swells and ridges. Beer advertisements are everywhere, the only good one a 3-D jumps-out-at-you Budweiser sign. Next to it are framed photographs of Clydesdales. A big glass of Bud costs $2, and pizza is cheap.

On Saturday evening, the bar was empty, with just a few men watching football on the big-screen TV. . . until the karaoke operators arrived at 10 p.m. They were soon followed by thick-armed blue-collar Southside men wearing sports uniforms with keys clipped to their belts and women dressed like the cast of Roseanne, in jeans that strangled ankles and sweatshirts with teddy bears.

The crowd loved its karaoke and clapped heartily after each performance. When not belting away Bob Seger, customers threw darts and shot billiards. Some were quite handy with a cue. A relaxed slouchy guy with a Nigel Tufnel hairdo couldn't miss. He was less successful with a microphone.

Despite my own outdated clothes, I was ruthlessly ignored, aside from a hefty loudmouth who called me a fucking Northsider. Obviously, everybody at the bar knows everybody else, and they don't need to know you. So just move into the neighborhood, get a job in a nearby factory and live here for twenty years, and I'm sure they'll eventually open up to you.

Dive Rating: 6

Zabornianka Lounge

5173 S. Archer Avenue (Archer Heights)
773-284-9707
*Hours: noon–2 a.m., Monday-Friday; noon–3 a.m., Saturday;
11 a.m.–2 a.m., Sunday*
Orange Line to Pulaski then transfer to the #62 Archer Ave. bus

The only Polish I know is zimne piwo. It means cold beer. So with no translator available, I was hard pressed to get the lowdown on Zabornianka Lounge, a Polish place in Archer Heights where English is rarely spoken.

It was New Year's Day, and the bar was still heavily decorated for the holidays, with strings of lights along the walls and two illuminated Santa Clauses guarding the cash register. Great red and green foil ornaments, one the size of a cocktail table, turned slowly in the air. More permanent fixtures included laminated counters and gold-patterned wallpaper.

Because it was the day after New Year's Eve, many customers were still dressed up from the previous night; many were still drunk. A woman with a bouffant hairdo and a sequined gown looked overdressed as she tapped at the video slots, and a boisterous carpenter nearly fell from his barstool. The efficient bartender was dressed in a power suit but would have been more comfortable in a laboratory coat. Her sharp appearance and calculated movements gave her an air of intelligence, as did her brainy head, the majority of which resided above the eyebrows. She spied an empty cigarette pack and in a single motion swiped it off the bar, tore off the pack's promotion and tossed it away.

The drunken man to my right spoke Polish like a somber cello, then, after realizing I couldn't understand him, tried to converse in labored English. A sentence took several minutes to finish and required outside help, but I eventually found out he was trying to say he didn't speak good English. And he had been in Chicago for thirteen years, his wife for thirty, and he would like to buy me a drink. I ordered a glass of Old Style ($1.25).

Get lost in another culture. Also stop by nearby Marzano's Miami Bowl, 5023 S. Archer Avenue. It is gloriously run-down, features eighty lanes of bowling and is open 24 hours a day, seven days a week.

Dive Rating: 6 ● ● ● ● ● ●

DOWNTOWN

LOOP
MAGNIFICENT MILE
RIVER NORTH
WEST LOOP

Billy Goat Tavern
430 N. Michigan Avenue (Magnificent Mile)
312-222-1525

Hours: 7 a.m.–2 a.m., Monday-Friday; 10 a.m.–3 a.m., Saturday;
11 a.m.–2 a.m., Sunday
All Loop bound trains deposit you within walking distance of this bar. On
the Brown, Green, Orange and Purple Lines, exit at State; on the Red
Line, exit at Lake; on the Blue Line, exit at Clark. Buses # 2, 3, x4, 10, 26,
143, 144, 145, 146,147, 151 and 157 also stop nearby.

Greek immigrant William Sianis opened the original Billy Goat Tavern in 1934 at 1855 W. Madison Street, across from the now demolished Chicago Stadium. He paid $205 for the bar—then called Lincoln Tavern—and the check bounced. He repaid with that weekend's earnings. Soon afterward a goat fell from a truck and walked into the bar. Sianis took a shine to the thing, grew a matching goatee and Billy Goat Tavern was born.

The bar's legend grew in 1945 when Sianis took a different goat, Murphy, to Wrigley Field to see the Cubs play Detroit in the World Series. Though Sianis had purchased a ticket for Murphy, ushers, and later Cubs owner P. K. Wrigley, would not let the goat into stadium. They said it smelled. In retaliation, Sianis conjured a curse: "Cubs, they not gonna win anymore." The Cubs lost the Series and haven't won it since. After the game, Sianis telegrammed Wrigley: "Who smells now?"

In 1964 Sianis moved his tavern to its current location beneath the Magnificent Mile. Back then, Chicago's five daily newspapers and four wire services kept the Goat filled with journalists. To this day enlarged bylines tout scribes who have swapped stories over suds at the Billy Goat. None is more legendary than the late Pulitzer-winning columnist Mike Royko. Of Sianis, he wrote, "He ran this tavern by stern rules: cash, no fighting, and printers from the newspapers weren't supposed to sit on the stools if they had ink on their pants."

After the Billy Goat was robbed, Royko questioned Sianis as to why he kept a goat and not a dog. Sianis answered that he once had a dog, but that it bit a customer, and he had to pay for the man's hospital bills. He then had to pay for veterinary bills when the dog got sick because the bum he bit drank martinis. "Besides if things got real tough, you can get milk from a goat," Sianis added. "You can even make a good stew from a goat. What can you do with an old dog?"

The bar gained additional fame when *Saturday Night Live* parodied Sianis and his Greek line cook in a skit whose catchphrase was "Cheezborger! Cheezborger! No fries, cheeps! No Pepsi, Coke!" To this day, line cooks badger customers into buying a double cheese and chips.

Billy Goat Sianis died in 1970, but his nephew Sam continues the bar's odd loveable traditions. Sam Sianis has tried unsuccessfully to break the Cub's curse by bringing goats to games, and he hosts presidential candidates when they're in town. He has decked the walls with enlarged newspaper clippings, now browned by age, and black-and-white photos of him holding Greek beauty queens.

I stop by every so often for a beer and a few innings of baseball. I usually find someone with something to say. Last time there I met an author, and we talked books for two hours. The bartenders wear aprons and also know how to gab. They are also seasoned professionals, as evidenced by the time one of them slid an open beer bottle down the bar to the dismay of my delicate heart.

Dive Rating: 1

Cal's Bar

400 S. Wells Street (Loop)
312-922-6392

Hours: 7:30 a.m.–7 p.m., Monday-Thursday; 7:30 a.m.–2 a.m., Friday; 7 p.m.–3 a.m., Saturday; 7 p.m.–2 a.m., Sunday (open Saturday and Sunday only if bands are playing)

Brown, Orange or Purple Line to LaSalle and walk west on Van Buren Street

The only real dive in the Loop, Cal's Bar—attached to Cal's Liquor—sits across the street from the pricey financial district but only charges $1.50 for a bottle of Pabst. A great deal whether you are a banker or a bum.

The crowd cuts across all lines—drunks, punks, bums, traders and students. After work, commuters down a stiff one then take a carry-out to drink on the Metro ride home. Bicycle messengers storm Cal's on Fridays (paydays), and the men's bathroom is plastered with their stickers and building security permits. During the day, the bar takes orders for neighboring Peppers Sandwich Shop. Just tell the bartender what you want, and he'll relay the message—and the sandwiches—through a small window in the west wall.

Cal's is a different kind of bar on weekends. I saw a guy with a mohawk, a woman in her wedding reception dress and a white-haired old-timer who drank from a 40-ouncer. A lonely San Franciscan bought me beer after beer then introduced himself to a group of women by trying to guess their shoe sizes. The bar stays open late on weekends and hosts bands, mostly punk. There is no stage, and speakers rattle on the bar's countertop. Band posters and old set lists are taped to the walls, and sometimes the musicians outnumber the customers.

I was drinking Blue Ribbon one night when Shakespeare shared his version of the bar's history. Shakespeare, a regular who has been drinking at Cal's since 1977, also answers to Shaky, Shaky-Poo, Shakymon, Hey You, Hey Schmuck and Hey Asshole. He said the bar opened in 1948, and he remembers when George—father of current owner Cal—used to run the place.

"I was here when the first piece of plaster fell," he said looking at the peeling ceiling. "It went right into my drink. I said to George, 'You're going to pay for this drink, right?' 'No,' he says. 'It was an act of God.'"

Dive Rating: 6 ⬤⬤⬤⬤⬤⬤

Cal's Bar

Rossi's

Hours: 7 a.m.–2 a.m., Monday-Friday; 7 a.m.–3 a.m., Saturday;
11 a.m.–2 a.m., Sunday
#29 State Street bus, the Red Line to Grand or the Blue, Brown, Green or
Orange Line to Clark & Lake

DOWNTOWN

Drinking in the morning has its drawbacks. It is strange to leave a bar in the daytime after you just told the bartender good night. Also, going to work smelling of gin isn't the best way to keep your job. And when the buzz wears off, you're tired and groggy and not in the mood to march for the Man. Best thing to do is call in sick and make a day of it. That said, I couldn't write about Rossi's with a clear conscience until I stopped in for a drink before work.

Rossi's opens at 7 a.m. and it's not unusual to see the place packed. However, the Monday I went it was dead—just me, the bartender and another guy who read his paper with a scotch and soda. Mornings near the end of the week tend to be rowdier, with alkies stopping in after breakfast to continue their binges. It's usually lively at night.

The bar has a log-cabin interior, a decent jukebox, beer for $2.50 and cocktails for $3. You can win pitchers with three bull's-eyes on the dartboard, but if your aim is off, a jug of Old Style will cost you $9. House rules include don't talk to Frank about Oleg Cassini (who he believes murdered JFK) and don't play "The End" on the jukebox. Springman, a local superhero who makes objects out of springs (spring underwear, for instance), is a frequent customer. Rumor has it he knows how to remove parking boots from cars.

CHICAGO'S BEST DIVE BARS

Of the crowd, a regular said, "You get business types, yuppies, low-lifes, hipsters, guys with beards to their knees and guys that buy vodka with quarters. It's great." He went on to tell me to keep an eye on my money. As he said this, an old drunk actually made for his cash. The bartender saw what was happening, and speaking slowly, as if conversing with a foreigner, told the old boy, "That's not your money." With the money in his hand, the old-timer stood there, confused. The bartender pointed to a nearby stool, "You're hat and your other belongings are over there." Eventually the money had to be snatched out of his hands. Defeated, he muttered and groaned, then plopped on his fedora and shuffled out of the bar.

Dive Rating: 6 ●●●●●

Second Story Bar

157 E. Ohio Street (Magnificent Mile)
312-923-9536

Hours: noon–2 a.m., Monday-Friday; noon–3 a.m., Saturday;
3 p.m.–2 a.m., Sunday
Near all Loop-bound El lines, but closest to the Red Line's Grand station.
A number of Michigan Avenue buses
(#3, #10, #26, #145, #146, #147, etc.) pass even closer.

In some ways, Second Story is the downtown bar I've always hoped for. It is a little classy, a little sleazy, hard to find and quaint. The bartenders are great, the music unconventional. (They played obscure show tunes the night I was there.) Look for a door with a sign for psychic readings, tucked between an Armenian restaurant and The Gap, enter and climb the stairs. After a red door and a twist and a turn, you'll find yourself in a cozy room that resembles a study, with burgundy walls, wood, a cleverly shaped bar and tinted windows facing Ohio Street.

Little lamps cast but little light, and when you sit down, be prepared to pay. Heineken costs $5. Luckily for me the bartender was fantastic, and when I asked for the best deal, he countered with "What do you like?" I ordered an old-fashioned with Maker's Mark, and he let me name my own price.

In other ways, Second Story is a nightmare, particularly if you are straight. All through the night, I needed both hands free to make sure others' hands kept to themselves. The actor to my right got the picture soon enough, but the playwright to the left, a nasty, pathetic man who lied about winning a Pulitzer, just wouldn't stop. When I told him I was straight, he yelled, "Then get the fuck out of here."

I went to the bathroom and found it locked. When the door opened, men tumbled out like clowns from a Volkswagen, followed by the sweet scent of weed. At a table in the corner of the back room, a man watched television as another man's head bobbed at his crotch.

Back in the barroom, I talked with a man in the art scene who described the city as a jelly doughnut. Bite into it and the sweetness bursts out. He told me I was smart and handsome and invited me out to Oak Park for a meeting of a gay and lesbian club. I hadn't heard of the group, and he asked if I was straight. My answer ended the conversation and my night at Second Story.

Dive Rating: 4 ●●●●

CHICAGO'S BEST DIVE BARS

The Sea of Happiness 640 N Wabash Avenue (River North)

312-787-2721

Hours: 11 a.m.–2 a.m., Sunday-Friday; 11 a.m.–3 a.m., Saturday
Red Line to the Grand stop

On one visit to the Sea of Happiness, construction workers with massive arms and tattoos of Old Glory told me about the day's adventure at their job site, a nearby high-rise. It was summer, and at mid-day some workers looked next door to find a man and a woman having sex on a condo balcony.

"You should have seen it," a man told me. "Cockman had her from behind and was just doin' her." Word quickly spread, and soon the whole crew, aside from one man and his friend who were working in the stairwell, ran over to the side of the building and did exactly what's expected of construction workers. They whistled and yelled. (The man in the stairwell said that though he saw nothing, he felt the tower lean as the workers rushed to watch the action.) One gentleman, head wrapped in the Stars and Stripes, said that Cockman's weapon was at least this big, and he held his hands apart at an admirable distance. "But that was through the binoculars. It must have been at least this big up close." The space between his hands widened to the size of a trophy trout. Perhaps like you, I thought, "They carry binoculars?"

On another visit, a carpenter with hands like hams told me about Johnny Rebel, his parrot. The carpenter said that for fifteen years he had been trying to teach the bird how to say, "Blow me!" It never took, though after his wife scolded the bird, the parrot piped back verbatim, "Johnny Rebel, you're a bad bird."

The Sea of Happiness shares its building and bathrooms with the Cass Hotel. I've seen a fashionable dandy strut through the door in designer jeans and stop dead. It being too late to turn back, he mumbled an order while his girl found a seat as far from the bar as possible—about fifteen feet away in this cozy joint. He gulped down his rum and coke ($4) and quickly scampered off, girlfriend in tow. The men all turned to watch her ass.

I don't usually stay too long, either. A couple of $2 Millers, or a pitcher for $7 and it's time to go. But I always come back. I love the dust-covered stucco walls and plastic crabs. I love the sentimental sketches of

Chicago, the letters painted on the windows and the way the Greek proprietor retires to watch TV in a storage closet just big enough for his E-Z chair. I love that it's the only bar I know where you can do your laundry—the machines are across the hall from the toilets—while you drink. And I love the safety of the life preserver that hangs behind the bar, "The Sea of Happiness" printed boldly upon it, ready to rescue thirsty barflies from the shitty downtown scene.

Dive Rating: 7 ⬤⬤⬤⬤⬤⬤⬤

The Sea of Happiness

T & T Lounge

184 N. Halsted Street (West Loop)
312-226-7173

Hours: 6 p.m.–midnight, Sunday; 8 a.m.–10 p.m., Monday-Wednesday;
10 a.m.–midnight, Thursday; 8 a.m.–2 a.m., Friday;
1 p.m.–3 a.m., Saturday
Green Line to Clinton or the #8 Halsted Street bus to Lake Street

In the up and up West Loop, T & T is a downright blemish.

In the mornings when trucks along Lake Street load and unload meat and produce, the gritty little bar fits right in. But as the neighborhood wakes up, luxury coupes and SUVs start to crowd the streets. By night, clubs coral crowds with velvet ropes, upscale restaurants squeeze in reservations, and galleries serve art with wine and cheese. Affluent young couples walk in out of warehouses, recently converted to luxury lofts.

But the T & T, a predominantly black dive, bucks all trends. While other bars serve martinis with blue cheese in the olives, T & T serves its gin with juice, disbursed in separate glasses for personalized mixing. Some drink from jeweled pimp cups, and a round might be accompanied with a bowl of ice. I watched as two ladies sipped shot glasses of Crown Royal backed with beer on the rocks.

I joined the fun with a Two Taylor Brothers ($9), a T & T special known to cause temporary blindness. It's a three-shot drink of gin, vodka and citrus-flavored light rum with a choice of mixer. I picked cranberry juice, but after all that booze, there was little room left for juice. Back-up juice was poured in a small, separate glass. I battled the Two Taylor Brothers with sips, trying to make room for more cranberry juice that would deaden the zing. I sipped and poured and sipped and poured some more, and by the time I had achieved a good mix, I was thoroughly pickled and the glass was still full.

As my sobriety yielded, a DJ stowed in a corner cubby rocked with I-want-to-take-you-home-and-give-you-my-love type jams, occasionally breaking into a track with corny commentary. The music played loudly enough to drain out the rattle of the El trains overhead. Some danced, squeezing between the bar stools and cocktail tables. A sign invited people to a soul food Sunday, chicken and chitlins included, and asked all comers, "Player or Playa?"

Dive Rating: 7 ●●●●●●●